Emily Chantiri

Every Day is Mother's Day

Find time, save money & reward yourself — without the guilt!

John Wiley & Sons Australia, Ltd

First published 2008 by
John Wiley & Sons Australia, Ltd
42 McDougall Street, Milton Qld 4064

Office also in Melbourne

Typeset in Charlotte 10.5/14.5 pt

National Library of Australia Cataloguing-in-Publication data:

Author:	Chantiri, Emily.
Title:	Every day is mother's day : find time, save money and rewar yourself - without the guilt / author, Emily Chantiri.
Publisher:	Richmond, Vic. : John Wiley & Sons, 2008.
ISBN:	9780731407576 (pbk.)
Subjects:	Women--Time management Women--Australia--Finance, Personal. Women--Life skills guides Self-management (Psychology)
Dewey Number:	646.70082

Cover design by Production Works

Author photograph © Keith Friendship/Monte Luke Studio

Cover image © iStockphoto/Royce DeGrie

Printed in Australia by McPherson's Printing Group

10 9 8 7 6 5 4 3 2 1

Contents

Acknowledgements v

Introduction vii

1 The little things really add up 1

2 Saving beauty 19

3 The lowdown on debt 35

4 Big-ticket items 53

5 Around your home 65

6 Teaching the children 95

7 Clothes and accessories 121

8 Money makes money 139

9 Healthy savings 161

10 The final word 175

Appendix: rewards for you 179

Index 183

To Daniel and Marc

Acknowledgements

Thank you to the team at Wiley for giving me the opportunity to write this book and bring it to life. To my family and friends, who supported me and shared my journey, and to all the mums who shared their stories, I thank you all.

Zen teaching tells us not to worry about the branches, but go straight to the root, because taking care of the roots takes care not only of the branches but also of the leaves, the flowers and the fruit.

Introduction

A mother's role today is a far cry from the traditional homemaking one of the 1950s and the decades before. These days, many mums juggle a career and a home life. Most take care of household bills, chauffeur their children from place to place and do the housework — the list is endless. Yet while we manage to 'do it all', we do very little for ourselves.

It doesn't matter if she is working or unemployed, or single or partnered, ask any mother what she wants more of, and she will answer, 'Time and money to enjoy some of life's pleasures'. Remember, while our circumstances differ, we all need to reward ourselves now and then.

We all want the best for our children; as parents, we want to make sure they receive the best education and opportunities life can afford them. It's so easy to fall into the pattern of putting our children first, but by doing so we forget about ourselves. Before this book was even an idea, I often had discussions with my female colleagues on this very topic. Some were good at taking time out for themselves while others were not so good at it.

Although we love our children dearly, at times it seems it's children's day every day. So I wrote *Every Day is Mother's Day* to help you regain some time and money that you can use to reward yourself without feeling guilty. It's now time to move yourself up on your list of priorities to ensure you make the most of your life. Remember that you don't have to give yourself a monetary reward. For a lot of mums, finding some 'me time' is reward enough. This could be something as simple as watching TV, soaking in a hot tub or taking time on a Sunday morning to sleep in and read the Sunday papers.

The first step in regaining some me time is to take a look at the areas in your life that you can cut back on in order to find money or time to reward yourself. Every chapter of this book takes you through ways you can cut back — whether they be related to your children, your home, your shopping or even your choice of beauty products. You'll find plenty of great tips to save, followed by examples of how you can reward yourself with your new-found savings. If you've neglected this area of your life, it will take a little effort to adjust to putting yourself first. If you're like many mums, you've probably forgotten how to do this — I know I had!

You'll find great advice that will help you in almost every area of your life. Some of my tips require only a little effort, but they all provide significant savings, so look out for them. Also watch for the 'mum to mum' boxes scattered throughout these pages. They provide fabulous suggestions on saving from women who juggle motherhood and a career.

Treating yourself is not about waiting for that one day in May each year when you allow yourself to enjoy being pampered by the kids. Embrace your new mindset: from now on every day is Mother's Day.

After all, a happy mum leads to a happier family life.

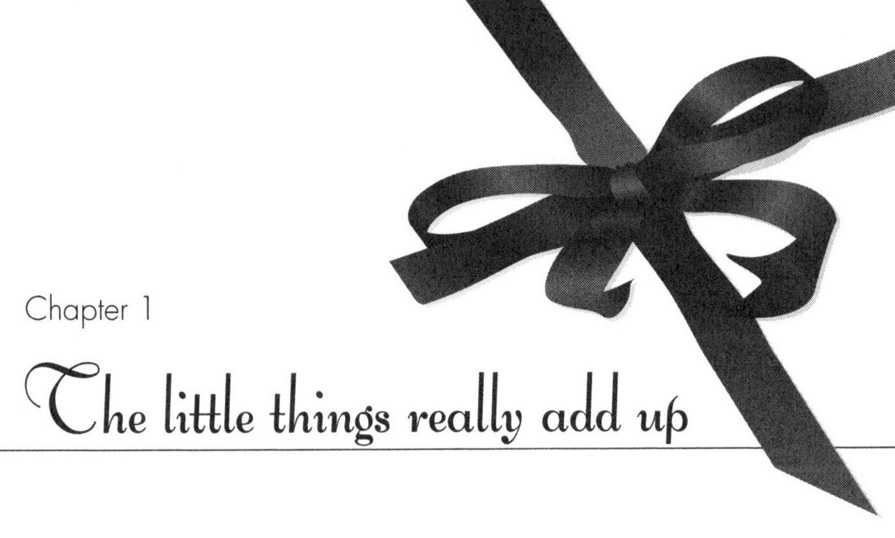

Chapter 1

The little things really add up

What better place to start cutting back than with the little things? We tend to take for granted the buying of everyday items. The danger lies in their prices being so low. When you're spending $2.00 here and $1.50 there, you tend not to notice. Although small purchases don't cost much on their own, added together, they provide you with a great opportunity to save.

By just buying fewer things, you'll be able to treat yourself with your savings. You may want to have a night off to go out to dinner, pay a babysitter so that you can see a movie or even do something simple, such as catching up with your girlfriends over coffee.

At the end of this chapter, you'll discover how you can eliminate nonessential spending and how the little things can make for big savings down the track.

Top tip: saving money at the ATM

This tip takes a little bit of forward planning, but it's an effortless way to save.

I know it's easy to pull up to any ATM and withdraw money, but did you know that you can be charged as much as $2 for using an ATM that isn't owned by your bank? The simple solution is to stick to your bank's ATMs. However, bear in mind that even if you use only those ATMs, once you reach your free-transaction limit for the month, you will probably have to pay up to $1.50 for every transaction after that.

So stick to your own bank and you will save up to $10 a month — giving you enough spare cash to share coffee and cake with a friend.

A little planning goes a long way

It sounds tedious, I know, but planning your finances really is essential. To do this well, you need to set a plan that is realistic and stick to the money-saving practices you implement.

We all need tools to help with organising ourselves. A budget planner is a useful tool for keeping your spending under control. There are dozens of planners online — why not download one from the internet? The consumer advocate organisation CHOICE has a simple one you can use (at <www.choice.com.au>). If you prefer to write things down, then grab a journal and keep a diary of your outgoings for the month. Either option is a great way to keep track of your money.

Learning to live within your means is important

Learning to live within your means is important. One way to do this is to carry a limited amount of cash each week. Calculate what you think you'll need, and then withdraw it one day a week only. You may like to choose the start of the week. The trick is to limit the number of withdrawals you make and keep within your budget.

Once you have withdrawn your money for the week, only carry what you need for each day, leaving the rest at home. Let's face it, if your wallet is full of cash, the temptation to spend it will be hard to resist. On the other hand, if you limit the amount of cash you carry around, you won't be as tempted to spend it; in fact, you'll find you spend less without even noticing.

Making your account work for you

While we're on the subject of banks, it's worth taking a look at your monthly bank statement if you want to save. In particular, examine the statement of the account that you use for most of your transactions. If you continually withdraw from it, be that for cash or paying bills online, make sure it gives you unlimited monthly transactions. You usually have to pay a fee of about $5 a month for this. However, that cost is minimal compared with the cost of going over a monthly free-withdrawal limit (which usually applies to accounts with no monthly account-keeping fee).

Accounts charging no monthly account-keeping fee give you a limited number of monthly free transactions, usually six. Once you exceed that limit, you are charged up to $1.50 per transaction.

So if you don't make many transactions, consider opening an account with a transaction limit. Of course, if you exceed your monthly limit, you may find yourself paying $15 in fees a month. Imagine if you did this for six months—you would have spent $90 in fees. Compare this with opening an account that gives you unlimited transactions for $5 a month—after six months you would save $60. The lesson here is that you should choose a bank account that suits your requirements.

Some good news

A breakthrough could be on the way for those annoying ATM fees, thanks to negotiations between the Reserve Bank of Australia (RBA) and the Australian Bankers' Association (ABA).

By October 2008, the RBA plans to abolish bilateral intercharge fees, which are charged to banks and other financial institutions by ATM owners for use of their ATMs. This should result in the reduction or abolition of the fees charged to ATM customers for using an ATM that isn't owned by their bank or credit union. With the fees abolished, ATM owners will still be free to charge an ATM customer, but the fee must be disclosed on the ATM screen before the customer can proceed.

Choose a bank account that suits your requirements

Although this is good news, the changes will not benefit everyone. Lower charges will apply to most major inner-city ATMs, but in regional towns customers may still be stung with high charges (due to the high costs associated with operating ATMs in underpopulated areas). Until this becomes official, watch out for those nasty ATM fees.

Penalty fees

Penalty fees really hurt your hip pocket. Penalty fees occur when your account does not have enough funds to cover a direct-debit transaction or a cheque you wrote, or when you go over your credit card limit or make a late payment. These annoying little fees can end up costing you as much as $50 a month. Have you ever been only a day out in balancing your accounts only to be hit with an overdrawn fee? It's so easy to do, particularly if someone deposits a cheque you wrote a long time ago.

Regularly check your bank statements. If you feel as though you have been unfairly penalised for a late transaction, then it's in your interest to phone your bank and ask it to reverse the charge. In most cases the bank will comply, particularly if you're a good customer and the late payment is a one-off occurrence. This happened to me not too long ago. When I rang the bank and explained the situation, it, luckily, reversed the charge. Don't let late fees cost you — you may as well grab a $50 note and tear it up for all the good these fees do you!

Fortunately, CHOICE <www.choice.com.au> has launched a campaign to have bank fees reduced, after hearing hundreds of negative stories from consumers. Thankfully, CHOICE's efforts have made headway: some banks are reducing their penalty fees, if not eliminating them altogether.

Also, if you have no luck convincing your bank to overturn a penalty fee, read the step-by-step guide to reclaiming your fees on the CHOICE website, at <www.choice.com.au>.

You've seen how the little things can really add up. No doubt there are probably other areas where you can cut back a little.

Bargain buys: getting your weekly gossip fix

If you've got to have your regular magazine fix, then take up a subscription. Most magazine subscriptions offer discounts of up to 40 per cent off a magazine's recommended retail price. Plus, many will throw in a bonus gift when you subscribe. To find more great deals on magazine subscriptions, visit <www.isubscribe.com.au>.

To give you an idea of how much you could save by buying a subcription, take a look at the following figures:

Six issues of a $7.95 monthly magazine	$47.70
Half-yearly subscription of the same magazine	$25.00
Saving	$22.70

Are lunches eating into your savings?

It's easy to form the habit of buying lunch everyday, particularly if you rush to get everyone out the door each morning. Yet making your lunch will make a big difference to your saving ability.

The savings in bringing lunch from home as opposed to buying it are quite staggering. Like in most households, you probably provide lunch not only for yourself but also for your children and partner. So encourage your family to make their lunches as well.

Top tip: cutting back on caffeine has more than health rewards

You can't leave this section without seeing the cost benefit of cutting back on the coffees you buy. It takes a small change in your lifestyle. Just take a look at the potential savings you could make if you only bought three coffees in a working week instead of five:

Five $3 coffees in a working week	$15
Three $3 coffees in a working week	$9
Saving	$6

Now take a look at what you'd save if you bought only three coffees a week, instead of five a week, over a year:

Five $3 coffees a week for a year	$780
Three $3 coffees a week for a year	$468
Saving	$312

You can see that by cutting out two coffees a week, you would save $6 a week, or $312 a year.

Now that's enough money for a cosy weekend away!

Let's look at the savings a household with two children and two parents could make if it purchased lunch three times a week instead of five:

Five $5 canteen lunches bought five times a week	$50
Two $5 canteen lunches bought three times a week	$30
Saving	$20

Two $7 lunches bought five times a week	$70
Two $7 lunches bought three times a week	$42
Saving	$28

The numbers show that you could save $48 a week, or $208 a month, by encouraging your family to make their lunches. Now here is the scary part: if you did this for a year, your family would save $2496.

With that amount of cash you could pay for a short holiday. Even better, you could use that money to have a night off from cooking dinner each week—and then go out for a meal instead.

Sandra's story, below, shows how she treats herself with the savings she has left over from making her family's lunches.

Mum to mum

I'm a single mum, and I found the rush in the morning to get my kids' lunches made for school was quite stressful, but I couldn't afford to give them money to buy lunches. Now I do a big grocery shop every two weeks and make sure I have enough food to make lunches. To help make things run more smoothly in the morning, I prepare the lunches the night before. I use a variety of fillings in the sandwiches, such as Vegemite, jam and peanut butter.

On the weekends I even make muffins and freeze them. I buy snack bars and small fruit-juice poppers to put in the kids' lunches. I take juice, muffins and a sandwich to work for myself. It really doesn't take long; you just need to plan ahead. I only do this Monday to Thursday. On Friday, as a treat, the kids are allowed to have a lunch order and I go out with my work friends for lunch. I don't feel so bad about this because I save on lunches throughout the week.

I find that saving money is very important, and so is saving time. It works really well for us all. Now we can all enjoy a 'lunch out' on Fridays.

Sandra, mother of two

As you can see, even changing how you do things in small ways will help you save money. Read the next section to find out how putting a little bit of money away will save you more than you would think.

Bargain buys: movie tickets

Don't pay full price for a ticket every time you go to the movies. Instead, purchase a book of five movie tickets and pay only $55. That's a saving of over $15 compared with buying tickets

Bargain buys (cont'd): movie tickets

individually. You can also purchase a book of ten children's tickets at discounted prices. On top of this, don't forget about the discount days offered by some cinemas; on those days the tickets prices are often reduced by up to 30 per cent.

Little things—big rewards

Now let's take a look at how putting a little away can make a big difference. Remember, no matter how much or how little you make, always save.

Jam jars and bottom drawers

When a friend of mine, Jacqueline, found out she was to become a mother, she started putting money aside. She took the change from her wallet at the end of the week and put it in a bottom drawer. At the end of each month, she took her savings and deposited them in an account she had set up for the purpose of her son's education. She did this religiously until her son was ready for university. After eighteen years she had accumulated enough to send her son to university. I still remember how proud she was when she told me this story.

Using this same method, you'll find that you can save for just about anything without hurting your wallet. Because you only put a little away, it's best to do this when you have a long-term savings goal. You can start with a smaller time frame than Jacqueline did, say, five years, and use your savings to replace your car or pay for a holiday. Diane uses some of her savings to take time off and catch up on some reading. See her story below.

Mum to mum

I take the morning off and go to my local cafe. I order a solitary coffee and actually catch up on glossy magazines, or I take a book. It's pure bliss.

Diane, mother of two

Once you have accumulated enough money at the end of the month, deposit the funds in your bank account. The two key ingredients to making this type of saving work are discipline and commitment, as Jacqueline showed. Open a separate bank account and differentiate it from your everyday banking account by naming it—for example, 'holiday account'. Your goal could be something as simple as saving for your yearly wardrobe or opening a rainy-day account that allows you to treat yourself. If you want to keep your savings in a traditional savings account only, make sure you open an account with no monthly bank fees. Seeing as you'll mainly be depositing into the account rather than withdrawing from it, you'll want an account without fees that eat into your savings.

Online savings accounts

Once you have accumulated enough money in your bank account, say, over $500, transfer this money into an online savings account. This is a smart move because you will maximise the return from your investment. Many online savings accounts offer returns of up to 7 per cent, which is high when compared with the 0.5 per cent return most banks offer.

Sarah opened an online account before her son was born. She uses the money to treat herself to regular massages. Read her story here:

Mum to mum

I opened an online account with ING Direct called a Savings Maximiser. It was really easy.

If ever I had some spare money, I would transfer it to my online savings account. By the time my son was born last year, I had saved just over $2000. I like the fact that I can withdraw money when I really need it. I can do this by transferring the money online into my normal bank account. It's more flexible than a term deposit, but it's not as tempting as having a normal bank account, because I don't have an ATM card to access the money. I receive around $120 in interest a year.

Until I get back to work, I have vowed not to let my savings fall under $1000. I have started using the money for regular back massages. After having my son, I suffered from chronic back pain and had to have regularly massages at $60 per session. Now I have just one a month; this is more about finding time out for me when I can relax. It's nice to know that if I want to treat myself, I know the money's there.

Sarah, mother of one

To see details of suitable online savings accounts, start with ING Direct (go to <www.ingdirect.com.au>) or BankWest (go to <www.abetterdeal.com.au>). You'll find more information on online accounts in chapter 8, Money makes money.

Fixed-term deposits

Fixed-term deposits are another option for you, because they deliver higher returns than normal bank accounts. Most banks offer deposits that return about 5.5 to 7 per cent on an investment of $5000. When you compare this with having your money sitting in a regular bank account that barely earns half a per cent, it makes sense to move your money to a term deposit, particularly if you're saving for a car or family holiday.

Fixed-term deposits ... deliver higher returns than normal bank accounts

The beauty of a fixed-term deposit is that you can open the account online, and its interest is calculated daily and then added to your account at the end of each month. (Putting your savings in a managed fund is also a savings option you should consider. Managed funds are covered in detail in chapter 8, Money makes money.)

Just by parking your money in a fixed-term deposit that has an annual rate of return of 7 per cent, you would earn a return of $350 on a $5000 deposit. Compare this with putting the same amount of money in a savings account returning 0.5 per cent — then you'd only receive a $25 return.

There is clearly no arguing about which option makes the most cents! You would have an extra $325 in savings if you invested the money in a fixed-term deposit. Indeed, even if you only put $1000 in the fixed-term deposit, you'd receive $70 in interest per annum.

One of the reasons fixed-term deposits are popular is that they are low risk and easy to obtain. Another advantage is that they don't tempt you to pull your money out so readily, because accessing money in them is more difficult than withdrawing from a regular bank account.

Having said that, withdrawing money from a fixed-term deposit is certainly not impossible. It generally takes only a phone call, and then the money can be transferred into a day-to-day account of your choice, usually within a day or two.

Ponder point

I think it's important for you to understand that you don't need to be the perfect mum. Just know there are a million ways to be a great mum.

Take the $5 challenge

As you read through this book, you'll find ways to give a little back to yourself. So to get you on the road to rewards, why not take the $5 challenge? To do this, take $5 each week and spend it on a treat for yourself, just like Rachelle did (read her story opposite).

Mum to mum

I started a $5 challenge as my weekly pick-me-up. I look for something for $5 to reward myself. It's amazing what you can find…I look for beauty products like nail polish and lipstick; I generally find them at discounted places, such as Priceline. The other day I bought a brooch at a market for $1.50. I went on my own, and I really enjoyed the time spent wandering around without the children. I set myself a target and bought the brooch, which was a lovely treat for me. When I'm at work, sometimes I splash out on a freshly squeezed Boost juice for $5. I figure that it's good for the inside and out. It makes for a well-deserved pick-me-up.

Rachelle, mother of two

The trick is to keep this process going by doing it regularly. Once you find more areas that you can cut back on, you may want to work your way up to spending, say, $10 a week on treats

Treat yourself

Sometimes just spending some money and time on the little things will give you the boost you need to face the week. Try some of these inexpensive little treats:

- *Share the cost of coffee and a slice of cake with a friend.* This shouldn't cost more than $15.

Treat yourself (cont'd)

- *Bring your own munchies to the movies, and go on a discount night when tickets are cheap.* This way, a movie shouldn't set you back more than $12.
- *Have your eyelashes tinted.* At a cost of about $20, an eyelash tint will not only make you look great but also allow you to not spend time adding layers of mascara in the morning.
- *Grab your diary and book two relaxing body massages within a six-month time frame.* (If you can afford more, then just do it.) Depending on your treatment, this will cost between $60 and $100.
- *Enrol in a short course at your local community centre or TAFE.* You may wish to try your hand at art classes, Pilates, meditation or even ancient history.
- *Buy fresh flowers on special every week for as little as $5.* It will add a splash of colour to your favourite room or even your work desk.
- *Phone a friend.* Spend at least fifteen minutes on the phone catching up with old friends each week. It's very important that you take time for yourself and that you spend it talking to another adult — sharing and supporting each other.
- *Update your music.* Buy a new CD or download inexpensive music from a legitimate source, such as iTunes (go to <www.apple.com/itunes>).

- *Book tickets to the opera or a play.* If you look for tickets towards the end of a show's run, you'll often find discounted tickets.
- *Stay in bed a little longer, and enjoy a slice of toast and a cup of tea before the day's activities begin.*

Chapter 2

Saving beauty

Do you remember a time when you thought nothing of having a regular massage, manicure or facial, or even of spending big dollars on the best beauty creams? I know I can — I bought the best products right up until the birth of my son. Then, suddenly, all the focus was on him and everything he needed. That's natural, of course, but by concentrating on all his needs, I forgot about all the ways I used to treat myself.

Even purchasing simple cosmetics was no longer on my radar once my son had been born. I found that rather than updating my lipsticks, I would just stick to the same ones I'd been using before he was born. Tragically, some fifteen years later I still have a few of those in the bottom drawer. (I'm sure I'm not alone here.) So now is the time to throw out old creams and make-up, and upgrade your look.

I know it can be a struggle to find the time, but some things only take a few minutes, such as painting your nails or giving yourself a pedicure at the end of the day while watching TV. As women, we are the masters of multi-tasking, so why not throw in something enjoyable just for you? It only takes a little bit of planning to find shortcuts in your day that will allow you to enjoy other things.

Take a look at the tips that follow for inspiration.

Online savings

By going online you'll no longer have to wait in line to be served at popular cosmetic stores or, even worse, feel pressured by sales assistants to purchase expensive products. Buying cosmetics online is quick and easy. Best of all, it offers real savings, because there is no store, or middleman, to cut into the profits. Most of the online beauty providers ship straight from the warehouse to your door.

By going online you'll no longer have to wait in line

Once you subscribe or become a member of these sites, you will usually receive a regular e-newsletter with all their specials—enabling you to save on your beauty needs. Best of all, if you order from Australian sites, you'll know the products you'll receive will meet Australia's strict pharmaceutical guidelines. If you buy products from overseas suppliers, you won't have consumer protection if the goods turn out to be fake or not licensed in Australia. This increases the risk of them being stopped by customs, which would waste your money.

There are dozens of online beauty suppliers. Below are a few Australian ones to start you off. For more local online beauty bargains, check out Annie Fox's *The Australian Shopaholic's Guide to Buying Online*, published by John Wiley & Sons.

- <www.perfume.com.au>
- <www.pharmacydirect.com.au>
- <www.thehealthandbeautyclub.com.au>.

Lesley shares her positive experience with using online discount chemists below.

Mum to mum

One really good money-saving tip I've stumbled across recently is using online discount chemists — they can save you a fortune.

Lesley, mother of two

Beauty bargains

Don't be fooled into thinking the most expensive beauty products work better than the cheaper ones. Consumer surveys have shown time and time again that the cheaper brands deliver results as good as the expensive ones.

As I mentioned earlier, before my son was born I didn't think twice about spending money on the well-known, expensive cosmetic brands, such as Chanel, Clarins and Biotherm. They're great products, but today skin-cream technology has advanced in so many ways that you no longer have to spend a fortune on moisturisers. For example, a proven winner with many women is Oil of Olay, priced at under $30; it delivers results to match those of the more expensive brands.

Ponder point

In order to practise what I preach about the importance of rewards, I decided a pedicure was in order. Walking past a beauty salon, I noticed that it was advertising pedicure specials for the day. 'Should I or shouldn't I?' I thought. The beauty therapist happened to be by the door of the salon and saw that I was reading over the specials. 'Come in', she said. I lingered a little further before walking in, thinking to myself, 'Just do it!'

For almost an hour, the therapist massaged, filed and scraped the skin from my feet. It was wonderful. While I enjoyed being pampered, I was offered herbal tea and a pile of glossy magazines.

I walked out with freshly painted, pink toenails and a smile on my face. Why did it take so long for me to make a decision? I took a while because I was not used to being rewarded. Once I thought to myself, 'Take one step at a time', a pedicure proved to be the ideal place to start!

As for face colour, Maybelline, Revlon and Rimmel offer great beauty buys in a range of hues. For instance, Rimmel's lipstick (priced at $9.95) and Maybelline's lipstick (priced at $11.95) deliver similar coverage and colours to the luxury brands. Watch out for specials on the cheaper brands. I recently picked up a Maybelline blusher that was on sale for just $6. By comparison, a mid-range blusher from an expensive brand can cost as much as $26. (Of course, if there is one brand that you have been using for years and that has just the right colour for you, just indulge.) If you're willing to cut back, try some of the beauty products that retail for about $10.

Bargain buys

Below you'll find some top-notch beauty products. They are all priced around the $10 mark.

Hair

- VO5 Hot Oil Shower Works ($5.00)
- Schwarzkopf Zero Frizz Hair Serum ($10.00)
- TRESemmé Vitamin E & Aloe Colour Revitalizing Shampoo and Conditioner ($10.00)
- TRESemmé Silk Shine Straightener ($8.00).

Make-up and nails

- Revlon Classic Nail Enamel ($11.95)
- Rimmel Mono Eyeshadow ($8.95)

Bargain buys (cont'd)

- Maybelline Expert Wear Blush ($13.00)
- Maybelline Great Lash Waterproof Mascara ($13.95).

Body creams

- Dove Firm Intensive Cellulite Gel Cream ($11.00)
- Vaseline Intensive Care Skin Firming Treatment ($8.00)
- St Ives Whipped Silk Intense Body Moisturizer ($6.00).

Tanning creams and sunscreen

- Palmer's Cocoa Butter Bronze Sunless Tanner & Instant Bronzer ($14.95)
- Garnier Ambre Solaire SPF 30+ (which protects against UVA and UVB, and prevents premature ageing, for only $13.00).

Hands and face

- Nivea Hand Intensive Nourishing Cream ($4.00)
- CoverGirl Smoothers SPF 15 Tinted Moisturizer ($14.50)
- Dove Protective Tinted Moisturiser ($9.00)
- Garnier Pure Deep Clean Cream Wash ($9.00)
- Nivea Visage Anti-Wrinkle Q10 (costs a little more at $17.55 but is very affordable when compared with other anti-wrinkle creams).

Multiply your make-up

Coming up are some cheap make-up tricks that are bound to stretch your beauty dollars further. For example, when you're running a little low on your favourite foundation, add a little moisturiser. This will not only make the foundation last longer but also provide you with the benefit of a moisturiser. Likewise, if you add some nail-polish remover to your nail polish and shake the bottle, you'll get even more use and prevent your polish from becoming gluggy.

Another good idea is to consider buying an inexpensive brown bronzer instead of brown eye shadow. You will receive much more product for your money, because you will be able to use it as an eyeshadow as well as a bronzer.

Also, here's a classic but often forgotten tip: shave with conditioner instead of shaving cream. It softens the hair, moisturises the skin and won't clog your razor. Alternatively, if you love using shaving cream, buy a standard men's version, which is usually cheaper and works just as well as women's shaving cream. Finally, go for moisturisers that have a built-in sunscreen.

A mother of three I spoke to, Becky, has a simple way to save time on make-up each day — shown here:

Mum to mum

One of the simplest make-up tips I've taken on is to use Vaseline as part of my beauty routine in the mornings. Vaseline has many uses, so it saves me not only money but also time. I use it to remove

Mum to mum (cont'd)

my eye make-up, and I often use it as a lip gloss in the colder months. Sometimes I even use it on my hands at night to keep my skin supple. It's cheaper than the beauty products out there and easy to locate. Another plus is that it works really well and doesn't irritate my skin the way many other beauty products do.

Becky, mother of three

Beauty treatments

If you're fortunate enough to live near beauty training colleges, it's worth checking them out for cheaper beauty services. They're always looking for models for their trainees and offering treatments for a fraction of the cost of those at professional salons. Even if you don't have one close by, it's worth finding one because the savings are significant — as Sandra's story, below, shows.

Mum to mum

I've come to terms with the [concept that] I was not giving to myself enough. I have discovered that I have given plenty to others and left myself out. After my marriage broke up, I began some introspection and discovered that I had put everyone first, although not on a conscious level. In the meantime, I'd forgotten about myself to the point that I realised I did not even know who I really was anymore or what I really wanted for myself.

I think women have been conditioned for generations, through both social and cultural conditioning, to put others before them. Before I got married, I would regularly have leg waxes, massages and facials. However, after the birth of my son, I felt guilty spending money on myself when I was not actually earning an income.

One day while I was at my local shopping centre, I saw a sign in the window of a beauty college that advertised student facials for very reasonable prices. At the time I noticed my skin was very dry and lacked that natural, healthy-skin glow, so I decided to book a facial. I received an hour-and-a-half-long facial for only $35, a fraction of the cost that I would normally have paid.

The students are in the last stages of their training, so they are ready to start to practise as beauty therapists. Also, there is always a supervisor on hand who consults with [the students] and oversees [their] techniques.

I've continued going to the beauty training school for a number of years now, and it's still great value. I make sure I book a treatment in every six to eight weeks. The other day I had a facial and a pedicure for $60.

Sandra, mother of two

By simply going to a beauty training college, Sandra was able to save $40 — almost half the cost of a $100 facial and pedicure given by a salon. Therefore, if she had six treatments a year at a beauty college, she'd save $240. She could then put those savings into more treatments, such as body massages or eyelash tints.

Top tip: having good foundation and concealer

Beauty experts all agree that the trick to having great-looking make-up is to start with a good foundation and concealer, so it may be worth spending more on these.

Hair

Hair products today are so sophisticated that colouring your own hair at home is easy. It's great to see products catering to the many women who don't have a lot of time. There are now a number of products available that enable you to touch up your hair colour in less than ten minutes. You'll find products to highlight, straighten and colour your hair from the comfort of your home. Mind you, every now and then it does feel good to simply let someone else do it for you, just as Maggie's story, below, demonstrates.

Mum to mum

I've been colouring my hair at home for years, but I needed a bit of pampering recently, so I decided to have my hair coloured professionally. It cost me $120, but I felt good and my hair looked great. Sure, it was more expensive than if I had done it myself (I only pay $15 for my store-bought hair colour). I decided I would [alternate between] colouring my own hair and going to a hairdresser.

Maggie, mother of one

Let's see how you could save money by alternating between colouring your hair yourself and going to a salon for it. Say that you buy a home hair-colour kit for $60 four times a year and see your hairdresser four times a year for $120 a session. When you add these figures up, it would cost you $720 for the year. Now compare this with the cost of visiting a salon eight times a year—you'd be paying $960 a year. This demonstrates that alternating between colouring your hair at home and going to a salon would save you about $240 a year.

Hairdressing colleges

Just as beauty colleges offer cheaper treatments, so too do hairdressing colleges. I've been to one where I had a cut and colour for only $60. That's an amazing saving—friends of mine pay up to $150 for the same treatment at a salon. Like at beauty schools, hairdressing colleges always have trained supervisors on hand to make sure that students are working correctly and customers are happy.

Now if you compare the cost of attending six $60 sessions at a hairdressing college (totalling $360) with the cost of attending six $150 salon sessions (totalling $900), you'll see that by going to the college you'd save $540. See the figures below.

Six $150 professional hairdressing treatments	$900
Six $60 hairdressing treatments at a college	$360
Saving	$540

Of course, if you really love your hairdresser but want to save some money, then you could alternate between seeing a professional hairdresser and visiting a hairdressing college. Let's work this out. If you went to a training college three times a year (costing you $180) and your professional hairdresser three times a year (costing you $450), you'd save $270. You could then take some of the savings you'd made from colouring your hair yourself and use it to receive a professional blow-dry.

Most hairdressers charge just $25 to wash and blow-dry your hair. The biggest advantage of a professional blow-dry is that it makes your hair look great and last a lot longer than if you had done it yourself. It is a great time saver, particularly if you've got a busy week ahead. I once had my hair professionally blow-dried for an event, and then didn't have to wash my hair for almost a week. It looked great the whole time and saved time in the mornings.

Break that down further and it cost me just over $3 a day to have great-looking hair for a week.

Knowing how to treat yourself

If you haven't had much time to think about pampering yourself, you're probably out of touch with the things you used to enjoy. Take a few minutes to make a list of the things you enjoy doing. You may like to include things that are often taken for granted, such as having time to yourself. Read Sonia's story, below, for an example.

Since the birth of my son, we have a rule where my husband takes our son out for a walk on Sunday mornings — so I can put a

treatment on my hair or face... That one hour he is out is time for me, and I really enjoy it.

Sonia, mother of one

Like Sonia, implement a rule in your household dictating that one Sunday of every month, you get to have a lie in — giving you the chance to read the papers and, if possible, have breakfast in bed.

Going on an early-morning walk is one of my favourite activities. It does take discipline, but I find it's a time of the day when I can take time out for myself, while exercising, and enjoy a coffee at the end of my walk. I also use this time to catch up with other friends. When I get back from my walk, I feel ready to get on with the day.

If you feel like something more luxurious, why not take off to a day spa? Read Helen's experience, shown below, of visiting a Korean bathhouse for a mum's perspective.

Mum to mum

I have to say that I'm really not big on indulging myself, but last year, my sister, my mum, my girlfriend and I decided to treat ourselves to a day at a Korean bathhouse. I'd never been in a situation in which everyone around me had stripped down. We were each given bathrobes, but we didn't use them because we were ushered, naked, into the shower prior to our treatments. We all enjoyed a hot bath, chatting away and forgetting about our nakedness. Then the therapist came through and took us to our

Mum to mum (cont'd)

treatment rooms. Our bodies were scrubbed and washed down before [we were] escorted away for a full-body massage. This was heaven. I had never felt so many miles away from my everyday life. It was so relaxing, and [the treatment] continued for about an hour. Once we finished our treatments, we couldn't help thinking that we had to do come back again. It was pure indulgence, but so well deserved.

Helen, mother of two

'Am I being selfish in taking time for myself? Am I being selfish in spending some of the family's hard-earned money on treats for myself? Couldn't I put that money towards paying off a little extra on the mortgage or putting a little more aside for the kid's education?' Do you ponder these questions when considering a treat for yourself? If you're worried about indulging in a few treatments, then think about it this way: As mothers, we are always giving to our children, husbands, families, communities and friends, and we take pleasure in doing so. So why not take pleasure in doing something for ourselves? I don't mean taking hours out of every day to indulge, but remember that a little fun goes a long way. A small treat every now and then does wonders.

Why not take pleasure in doing something for ourselves?

Rewarding yourself is empowering — when you're feeling good about yourself, your children, your partner and others notice it too. Plus, when you're feeling refreshed and on top of the world, more good things come your way. Remember, it's important that you take time to slow down, meditate and breathe in silence. Love the seconds and the minutes.

Treat yourself

When you're feeling like you need a lift, find ways to reward yourself for everything you do. You could:

- *get a manicure or pedicure, or a new nail or lip colour for the next season.*
- *splash out and get an instant tan at a spray-tan solarium.* (There's nothing like a bit of colour on your skin to lift your spirits.)
- *refresh your scent by splurging on a new fragrance.*
- *apply a do-it-yourself facemask or heat treatment on your hair.* These are things you can do while making dinner or doing the ironing. You can purchase the beauty products cheaply from cut-price chemists.
- *freshen up your smile.* Invest in some teeth-whitening toothpastes or formulas. Try CleverWhite or one designed for smokers, such as White Glow, which normally retails under $4.

Chapter 3

The lowdown on debt

Now that you've seen how some of the little things can have an impact on your finances, it's time to look at how you can reduce your overall debt.

Although a little unconventional, some of the tips in this chapter will help you pay off thousands of dollars over the years. Read on and see.

The mortgage

Imagine not having a mortgage to pay. What a huge relief it would be. Friends of mine who no longer have a mortgage hanging over them say that it's a huge release and that it gives them more time to spend on the things they like.

So how can you pay off your mortgage quickly? Well making additional mortgage payments or fortnightly repayments will fast-track this. When you pay off your mortgage fortnightly, you are effectively making 26 repayments a year compared with twelve repayments a year. In fact, if you make 52 weekly repayments a year instead of 48 (the weekly equivalent of making twelve monthly payments a year), you'll chip away at your mortgage even faster.

You can save thousands on your mortgage just by making extra payments and doing it often

Let's use an example. Imagine that you are paying off a $250 000 mortgage by making monthly repayments of $1831 at 7.4 per cent interest. If you paid this fortnightly at $916, you'd save about $69 370 off your loan and knock almost five years off its 25-year term (the standard term for a home loan).

You can also save thousands on your mortgage by making extra payments and doing it often. Take this as an example: let's say that you borrowed $250 000 for your mortgage at an interest rate of 6.5 per cent. If you made an extra payment of $50 a week, you'd save a huge $69 351 over the period of your loan. The best thing about this is that you would pay off the loan in less than 25 years — knocking five years and nine months off its term.

Both of these examples show you simple ways to shave thousands off your home loan. Remember, a saving of almost $70 000 is not to be sneezed at!

Top tip: acknowledge each milestone with a reward

Use milestones to reward yourself. For example, each time you pay off a chunk of your mortgage, give yourself a treat. Why not organise a night out with your partner while you have the kids looked after by a babysitter? After all, paying off a mortgage is a great achievement.

Use $5000 or even $10 000 milestones. When you pay off an even larger amount, take yourself and your partner away for a weekend.

Tips for selecting your home loan

When it comes to selecting a home loan, there are things you need to consider. Before committing to a specific loan, check that:

- *you can make extra or fortnightly repayments without penalty.* This is particularly important at the start of your loan when the interest makes up a large part of your repayments.
- *the low introductory rates, or honeymoon rates, on offer will benefit you in the long run.* Good interest rates may only apply for the first few months of your loan; then, when there is a rate rise, you could end up paying more than you would for a standard-rate loan. So make sure you know the rate that will apply once the loan's introductory period finishes.
- *your loan structure will suit your needs.* If you've applied for a variable loan, will you be covered if interest rates rise? Can you extend the term in case of financial difficulty? Make

an appointment with your bank manager to negotiate a better rate.

- *fees and penalties won't hold you back.* A loan with a high exit fee or penalties for making extra repayments could lock you into the loan — preventing you from finding better deals elsewhere.

Review your mortgage regularly. If you feel you're not getting the most from your mortgage, it could be worth visiting a mortgage broker. A mortgage broker will liaise between you and mortage bankers. A broker will shop around to obtain the best rate and loan term available to you. Once the loan is secured, you pay the broker a placement fee.

Making your home work for you

Okay, although there is no magic cure for making your mortgage disappear, you may want to consider options for generating income from your home. Some of the ideas in this subsection will help you earn income from your bricks and mortar.

Letting out a spare room

Renting out a spare room is a simple way to earn income. Try bringing in a student or boarder. Most people can expect to receive about $80 to $100 a week from letting out a room. It is a great way to add to your mortgage payments or, even better, have some extra cash to spend on yourself. Another bonus of having a boarder is that the income derived from doing so is not taxable. However, what you spend on maintaining a boarder's room is not tax-deductible.

If you have the room and don't mind having an extra person in your space, then the extra money could go a long way. Take this situation, for example: if you took in a boarder for six months and charged $400 a month, you'd earn a staggering $2400. Best of all, that amount wouldn't be taxable! See Sandra's story, below, for a real-life example.

Mum to mum

After my husband left, I stayed in the family home with my two children. We have a large home with four bedrooms.

It was my sister who suggested I get in a boarder such as a local student or a foreign exchange student looking for a place to stay while studying English. I recalled that one of the Japanese colleges in my area were after homes for their foreign students.

We ended up renting to a lovely, young Japanese girl, who was fantastic. I supplied the meals most nights, but she would look after the kids for me and clean around the house. She paid $80 a week for her board, and was a blessing for me and my kids.

Sandra, mother of two

Another option for you to consider is having a student stay with you for free in return for help around the home and with the kids. Now that's a real treat. My girlfriend Diane did just that. Read her story overleaf.

Mum to mum

I had a German girl stay with us for a few months while she was over here learning English. In return for free room and board, she did 25 hours of housework and child care a week. I had plenty of room anyway, so it was a great deal. She fitted in perfectly. The kids loved her. We were all very sad when she left.

Diane, mother of two

Using your garage to your advantage

Another way to maximise the returns on your home is to rent out your garage, particularly if you live in a high-density area with very little car space. Newspapers often include ads from people wanting to let out their garage. Consider doing a letter drop in your area advertising your garage space for rent. You could net $50 a week from it.

Speaking of garages, you can't ignore the benefits of putting on a good old-fashioned garage sale for extra cash. Get rid of all your clutter and unwanted baby furniture, and make a little money in return. You can expect to earn anywhere from $100 to $300 — not bad for a day's work! Or, if you don't want the hassle of organising a garage sale, sell the items on eBay (go to <www.ebay.com.au> to place an ad). Discard your unwanted stuff and, in the process, create room in your home for something new and special.

Making your home a star

Have you ever wondered where the sets for TV commercials and movies come from? Well many are found in ordinary homes across the nation. If you think your home has something to offer, consider making it a star. Film roadies are always looking for locations for film, TV and advertising shoots. Contact film and TV production companies to see if your home could provide a suitable set for a TV show or movie. For them, the condition of your home is not as important as it being easily accessible by film crews.

This strategy is exactly what a friend of mine used, and she earned $6000 from it! After hearing that a house in her area had been used for a number of television shoots, Angie decided she would contact film-location scout Bighouse to see if her home would make a suitable set. Read her story below.

Mum to mum

It was my neighbour who gave me the idea of renting my home [to a TV or movie crew]. My neighbour's home is quite unique and large, has plenty of bathroom space and has many rooms with dual access. The film crews liked the fact that they could shoot from all angles and fit all their equipment. My partner's and my home is large, so I thought we might have a chance.

So far, our home has been used twice. It's great; all you need to do is be out of the home for the day. We were paid $3000 for each shoot. During the filming they damaged a wall.

Mum to mum (cont'd)

The very next day they sent around a repair man who fixed the hole and then proceeded to paint the wall ... It was fantastic. He matched the paint perfectly.

Angie, mother of two

Imagine receiving $2500 or even $6000 from doing this. Yes, you could put the money back into the mortgage, but you could also use the money to do something for you, such as taking a course!

Credit cards

You'd be hard-pressed to find a person who doesn't own a credit card. It's hard to get by without a credit card these days, particularly for online purchases and paying for things overseas. The truth is, we need credit cards — they allow us the freedom to buy things when caught short. Plus, if someone steals your purse with your card in it, it's usually relatively easy to put a 'stop' on your card. By contrast, it's just about impossible to recover a purse full of cash.

I've always believed the problem with credit cards is that when you make a transaction, you don't actually see cash exchanging hands. Imagine that you have $500 in your purse. With each purchase you make, you will see the money dwindling; once there is no more cash in your purse, you will be forced to stop spending — simple. With credit cards, the money you're spending is invisible to you: you hand over your credit card and the friendly salesperson returns it intact. Nothing is lost, and you have plenty to gain as you happily walk out of the store with your bags of goodies — until the dreaded bill arrives!

Interest

It's very important to check that the interest rate on your credit card isn't too high. If you pay anything over 14 per cent interest, it's time to change cards.

Perhaps a 'financial health' alert that is similar to warnings about smoking and gambling, such as the one below, should be imprinted on your credit card?

Warning: overuse of credit cards can cause bankruptcy

Doing the sum

Let's imagine that you're carrying a credit card debt of $4000 and paying about 14.9 per cent interest. Provided you don't make further purchases, the interest payments alone will cost you $596.

However, by simply changing to a credit card with a lower interest rate, you will save hundreds of dollars a year. At the time of writing, Virgin was offering a credit card with no annual fee and an interest rate of zero for the first six months — rising to an interest rate of 2.99 per cent after that.

By rolling over a $4000 credit card debt to a Virgin credit card, you'd reduce your interest payments to about $119.60.

Compare this with the $596 payable on a credit card charging interest of 14.9 per cent. That's already a saving of $337, just by swapping cards and filling out an application, which only takes a few minutes.

If you would like to compare credit cards, visit <www.infochoice.com.au/banking/creditcards/compare/tables>.

Debt versus savings

If you have savings but are carrying debt on your credit card, paying off that debt with those savings is a wise move. I understand the benefit of having a savings plan. However, a credit card debt will eat into all your hard-earned savings because you will pay the interest on the card out of your potential savings.

For example, let's say that you have $2500 in an interest-bearing savings account that pays 6.5 per cent annually. This would equate to an extra $163 earned, and give you a total account balance of $2663. However, if your credit card was carrying $2500 from month to month and you were paying 16 per cent interest, the interest charged for the year would be $400. That $400 would erode your savings. So the $2663 in your bank account would actually be worth $2263, because you would have to use $400 of your savings to pay off the credit card debt.

Credit card reward programs — a privilege or not?

Credit card reward programs enable you to earn points for purchases you make on your card. These points can then be redeemed for discounts on travel and accommodation, and many other services and products. Credit card reward programs can work really well, as long as you are the one who is benefiting from them.

Beware that you can be charged $55 or more a year just to be part of a card reward program.

Frequent flyer points

By far the most popular credit card reward programs are those that allow card users to earn frequent flyer points when they make purchases. They can then redeem those points for discounted flights and other services provided by an affiliated airline. Typically, you can expect to use about 20 000 points to pay for a Sydney to Melbourne flight. This means you will need to have spent about $20 000 to earn those points, assuming you earn one point for every dollar you spend.

In this era of cheap domestic flights, the [frequent flyer] points you earn will barely cover a domestic flight

Although you can earn some frequent flyer points when you make everyday purchases, the best and most common way to obtain points in a frequent flyer program is to fly with your card's affiliated airline. Most programs reward travellers with a specific number of points based on the distance travelled.

If you have a large credit card bill every month and can see the benefits of the points you earn, then you may feel the fee you're being charged to join the program is justified. However, in this era of cheap domestic flights, the points you earn will barely cover a domestic flight, so it may not be worth your while.

Take a look at this example of what it would cost you to join a frequent flyer program on a credit card charging 18.25 per cent interest (typical for a frequent flyer card) and carrying a debt of $2500 over a year:

Interest charges	$456.25
Frequent flyer program charge	$55.00
Annual fee for card	$40.00
Total costs	$551.25

With stiff competition between airlines and discounted fares continually being offered, $551.25 can often be used to pay for two Sydney to Melbourne flights. Plus, if those flights aren't subsidised by frequent flyer points, they will almost certainly be subject to fewer conditions than flights booked using frequent flyer points.

Other types of schemes

As mentioned, credit card loyalty schemes can be used to receive discounts on all sorts of purchases. This can be very worthwhile, especially because the range of products on offer just keeps expanding. If you own a car, then it may be a good idea to sign up to a credit card loyalty program that offers iscounts on green slips and other types of insurance. You can also redeem points to snare special deals on household appliances, wine and other items with some cards.

Redeem points to snare special deals on household appliances, wine and other items

Rina is one mum who knows how to reward herself with her reward-program benefits. Read about her experience below.

Mum to mum

I find the vouchers I can get from Westpac Altitude are fantastic. My credit card's annual fee is $60, and if I don't rack up any interest, that fee is all it costs me. Usually, by November each year I have enough points to receive about $300 worth of Myer or David Jones vouchers. I use some of these to splurge on myself, and because I receive the vouchers close to Christmas, I see them as a Christmas bonus. I sometimes buy extra nice stuff or a few special treats, such as gorgeous Christmas decorations, table runners, and other new things that I like to have for Christmas day.

Rina, mother of two

However, don't become trapped by spending big just to earn redeemable points. See the points as a bonus, and use any vouchers you receive from the program to buy something special for yourself. Make your card work in your favour. Helen does this. See her story below.

Mum to mum

I have a credit card with a loyalty-points scheme, and the points can be redeemed for a big range of vouchers (for magazines, lingerie chains, hardware chains, the big department stores, theme parks and all sorts of other things), or for a rebate on travel,

Mum to mum (cont'd)

accommodation, insurance (car, home or health) or financial charges. I receive one point for every dollar I spend.

The card costs me $59 in annual charges, and the points can be redeemed once I have 1600 points. Most of the things I want require about 7500 to 8000 points, which cover a $50 car insurance rebate or $50 David Jones voucher, for instance. I definitely wouldn't use the card just to accumulate points, and I make sure I pay it off each month. I know it's not smart to spend a lot simply to get points. I see the points as a bonus, and I can use them to spend on vouchers in stores. The way I use the card, I can earn enough points to receive $100 vouchers twice, if not three, times a year.

Helen, mother of two

Don't forget to use your loyalty points to reward yourself. You spend your own money to pay bills and earn your own points, so balance this out with a small treat. You could use your vouchers for something as basic as new stockings, undies, a book or even some lovely stationery. Or, use your vouchers to buy a treat for someone special in your life.

Make your credit card work for you

To make the most of your credit card, you need to understand what you shouldn't do with it. So that you don't become trapped, never:

- *take up an unsolicited offer to extend your credit card limit.* Don't take up the offer, no matter how much the bank encourages you, particularly if you find it difficult to pay off the full amount of your debt each month.

- *rob Peter to pay Paul.* That is, don't play tag between existing credit cards by paying one card with another.
- *withdraw cash from your credit card.* Interest is charged immediately when you do this (even if your card offers interest-free days on goods purchased), and it can quickly hike up your interest payments each month.
- *make late or minimal repayments.* If you do this, you could be liable for a penalty payment of between $25 and $35 a month.

There's no point in having a credit card if it is dragging you further into debt or stopping you from receiving its full benefits. When it comes to choosing the right card for you and using it in the right way, you should:

- *use the power of negotiation.* Due to more people transferring their credit card debt to another card to receive a better deal, major financial institutions are becoming surprisingly willing to negotiate to keep customers. The CHOICE website <www.choice.com.au> has a number of success stories attesting to this, including many from consumers who negotiated to have an annual credit card fee waived or other costs lowered. It's worth checking out the site to pick up some negotiating tips.
- *jot down in your diary or organiser the purchases you make on credit.* That way, you'll have an idea of what you'll have to pay back before your bill arrives.

- *check your statement carefully.* Do this to make sure there are no nasty surprises or overcharged purchases on your bill.
- *find out if your credit card matches the benefits of others.* Visit the Cannex website <www.cannex.com.au> to do this. Cannex is an independent financial-services research group that provides free information on a number of financial services and products, including credit cards. Its credit card star-rating guide will help you find a credit card that suits your lifestyle.
- *remove the temptation to spend.* A credit card is like most other things in life: if you don't have it, then you won't miss it. If your goal is to pay off your credit card bill, then consider cutting up the card — knowing that you can, of course, always apply for a replacement card. Or, if that's too drastic for you, give the card to a trusted friend or family member until you have paid off your debt.

Debit cards

Debit cards are becoming increasingly popular. It's easy to understand why when you consider that with each year the debt carried on Australians' credit cards increases. Debit cards work extremely well for people who struggle to pay off credit card debt.

They carry all the functions of credit cards: you can make purchases online or over the phone with them. The difference between a debit card and a credit card is that the money used for payment in a debit card transaction is drawn directly from your savings account. This means you can monitor your account balance and see exactly how much money you have left to spend.

Check out Kristen's experience with debit cards; it is shown in the box below.

Mum to mum

A few years ago I maxed out my credit card for a few months, and was paying about $100 a month in interest. I would like that money back. A debit card would be good because it would allow me to access VISA functions while limiting me to spending only what I have in my account.

Kristen, mother of two

I hope this chapter has shown you ways you can reduce some of the debt hanging over your head. Remember, it's important to check all the fees and conditions on any loan, credit card or reward program before you commit.

Treat yourself

Remember, people need to do something for themselves now and then. Try one of these inexpensive rewards:

- *Diarise each time you've paid $5000 or more off your mortgage, and lock in a special night out or a weekend away to reward yourself.* (See the top tip on page 37 for more on savings milestones.)

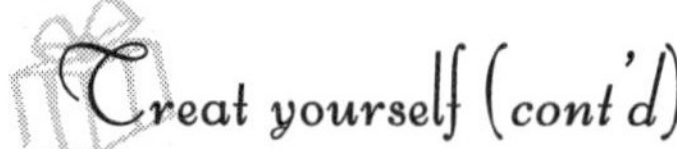

Treat yourself (cont'd)

- *Beautify your home.* This could be as simple as buying plants or an unusual piece of art that you have been eyeing off.
- *Purchase a new couch or dining table with the money you've saved.* Of course, if you don't wish to spend that kind of money, buy some lovely throw cushions.
- *Buy new towels to freshen up your tired bathroom.*
- *Invest in some glossy interior magazines for some decorating ideas.* Remember, a large rug or a lick of paint gives a home a great lift — and don't forget to pay attention to your home's outdoor areas.
- *Buy flowers to make your home feel welcoming.* Walking into a fresh-smelling home feels particularly nice after a day at work. Incense and other oils work well too. It's all about creating an environment that you look forward to coming home to.
- *Take a course in interior design.* A number of colleges offer short interior-design courses for novices wanting to make the most of their homes.

Chapter 4

Big-ticket items

In this chapter you'll find ways that you can cut the costs of big-ticket items. These can include expenses you pay once a year, such as your insurance or a holiday, and ongoing expenses.

Cars

Because your car probably forms a big part of your everyday life and can cost you in petrol, insurance and repairs, it really pays to learn how you can save on your car expenses. This section shows you how you can snare the best deal when buying your vehicle and insurance. Watch out for the top tips, which give you further ways to reduce your expenses.

Bumper to bumper sales

Today used cars have never been cheaper or more affordable, thanks to an oversupply of cars in the marketplace. I'm not suggesting that you buy a car that is many years old; you can save as much as $5000 if you buy a car that's only six months old. Good-quality second-hand cars are selling for prices much lower than those of brand-new cars.

The best place to buy cars is an auction. I've done this, and it saved me more than $5000 compared with my buying a car privately or through a dealer. It pays to take someone along to the auction who has some knowledge of cars, because it's worth every cent saved. Make sure the car you're considering buying has its entire service history and logbooks. This will tell you how well the car was maintained by its previous owners. To see the vehicles for sale at car auctions, visit <www.pickles.com.au> or <www.themotorauction.com.au>.

To help you choose the right car for your lifestyle, there are some great sites designed to take some of the hassle out of buying a car. The following car-sale websites allow you to compare car prices and features, and they have reviews on the various models:

- <www.carpoint.com.au>
- <www.carsguide.com.au>
- <www.drive.com.au>.

Top tip: asking for help

I understand how difficult it can be to buy a car, so if you want to save time and money, visit <www.privatefleet.com.au>. The team at Private Fleet will do the haggling and paperwork for you for about $70. You can choose from new or used cars and save thousands.

Car insurance

One of the best things about the web is that you can use it to easily and quickly find the best comprehensive car insurance. For example, the first time I shopped around for car insurance, I saved $400 off my yearly premium. When I shopped around again, I saved another $100. So in as little as five minutes, I was able to save another $100 on my car bills. The way I see it, that saving constituted almost two to three weeks of free motoring, because that's what I spend in petrol — a great saving.

Top tip: insurance savings and shortcuts

Many insurance companies offer discounts and incentives if you have more than one policy with them. It really does pay to shop around though. The best deals allow you to package your home and contents insurance with your car insurance.

Also, it may suit you to pay your premiums quarterly or twice a year. Some insurance deals even offer a monthly payment option. These types of payment options can be beneficial if you don't want to

Top tip (cont'd): insurance savings and shortcuts

be hit with one large sum for the year. At times I've preferred to pay twice a year, rather than paying one big annual bill. It's comforting to know these options are available, particularly when money is tight. Bear in mind, however, that you may be charged for the option of paying for your insurance in instalments.

The Cannex website, at <www.cannex.com.au>, gives you a breakdown of the best comprehensive car insurance policies based on your age and driving history. Check it out to find the best deal for your needs.

Be aware of the budget insurance companies out there. Visit <www.budgetdirect.com.au> and <www.justcarinsurance.com.au>.

You may also want to look into the 1st for Women Insurance Agency at <www.1stforwomen.com.au>. The company sells car insurance to women based on the philosophy that low-risk drivers, such as women, should not have to subsidise high-risk drivers by paying expensive premiums.

Top tip: driving your car dollars further

Make the money you spend on your car go further by:

- servicing your car regularly so that it runs better and has better fuel consumption (up to 20 per cent better)
- using your air conditioner less (there is no doubt that we need air conditioning in summer months, but be aware that

havng the air conditioning on reduces your fuel economy by 10 to 20 per cent)

- keeping your tyre pressure at the recommended level and taking heavy items out of the car when you're not using it
- buying car accessories such as dash mats and seat covers to protect your car and help maintain its value.

Petrol

Due to rising fuel prices, it is now even harder to run a car economically. So find out the best days for cheap petrol in your local area. Prices generally fall on a Tuesday or Wednesday and rise just before the weekend.

Petrol prices can vary by up to 10 cents a litre, which means a drop in prices could save you $6 a tank. If you combine that discount with a Shop-A-Docket giving you 4 cents off a litre, you could save as much as $8.40 a week, and even more if your car has a big petrol tank. Based on these figures, you could save up to $436.80 a year. The box below demonstrates the savings busy mum Jenny makes by doing this.

Mum to mum

I'm really glad that I'm vigilant about the days I put petrol in the car. Sometimes I've seen the price go up by as much as 10 cents [at other times during the week]. When I do my calculations on a full tank of petrol, that discount saves me over $6. I always keep Shop-A-Docket petrol discounts in my car so that I can maximise

Mum to mum (cont'd)

my petrol savings. It's so worth the effort when you consider that you could save over $400 a year.

Jenny, mother of two

If you're unsure where the cheapest petrol supplier in your area is, visit this website for help: <www.motormouth.com.au>. Hopefully, you will save not only money but also time, because you won't need to drive from one petrol station to another looking for the best deal.

Holidays

One of the things I've come to cherish is a holiday. It doesn't matter if it's a weekend or a week away, as a holiday approaches I literally count down the days. Most family holidays are expensive. Because of this, we tend not to have them as often. Yet spending time away with your children is something you will cherish and later look back on fondly. A holiday allows you to let your hair down and relax, without having to worry about work or chasing homework.

This section includes some money-saving strategies you can use to cut the expense of your holiday.

House-swap holidays

Have you ever wanted your holiday destination to feel like a home away from home? Well that's what home-swap holidays offer — not only across Australia but also around the world. In a home-swap arrangement, you can trade your home with someone else's for an agreed period of time. Depending on the timing and your choice of holiday destination, you may just score five-star accommodation.

Once you become a member of a home-swapping website, you can book a place on it by emailing the member whose home you would like to stay at. Once you have both agreed on the date you wish to swap homes, an agreement is drawn up. The agreement is automatically generated by the website and then sent to its head office. Contacts usually cover all requirements, including bills, such as phone charges, to be paid. You can even stipulate in the agreement that you are happy to swap cars as well as homes.

Lauren and her husband, Jim, are members of a house-swap organisation. Lauren relates their experience below.

Mum to mum

We've traded our home six times and travelled to a number of places in Australia — including up north to Maroochydore and a farm stay in Victoria. We've enjoyed a two-week holiday in Adelaide, before swapping our home again for a fabulous villa in Perth.

We have been members of a house-swap site for a few years now, and because we have two boys, we tend to look for larger homes. There is generally plenty of information on the homes online, including details about nearby amenities, parks and playgrounds. I'm quite fussy, so I do spend a fair amount of time giving our home a thorough spring clean before we leave. I also make room

Mum to mum (cont'd)

in the wardrobe for the guest's clothes. Apart from the travelling costs, it's a great way to save money on a holiday and see another part of the world.

Lauren, mother of two

Before you decide to do a house swap, there are a number of things you need to check. They include the following:

- Make sure that your home is adequately insured, and confirm the level of your coverage.
- Check that you are covered for additional drivers' insurance if you intend on swapping cars as part of the trade.
- Lock away all valuables.
- Appoint a friend or neighbour to 'check in' on your home to make sure that everything has been taken care of and that your tenants have all they need.

If house swapping interests you, visit <www.houseswap.com>, <www.homeexchange.com> or <www.aussiehouseswap.com.au>.

What a difference planning makes

We all know how expensive it is to travel during the school holidays. So if possible, travel outside of school-holiday times. I know this is a lot harder if you have children because it can be difficult to take them out of school, but if your children haven't started school yet, take advantage of the cheaper travel available during the school term. If you travel prior to the last week of school and just before the school holidays start, you can almost cut your travel bill in half. Diane relates her experience with this in the box below.

Mum to mum

I live on the Gold Coast and have a lot of friends who visit my family and me regularly. They try to come up the week before the school holidays start. One time they were charged about $450 for five days' accommodation, and the following week it went up to almost $2000 because the school holidays had begun.

Diane, mother of two

Book airfares in advance, however, because the more time you leave between booking and flying out, the cheaper your fares will be. Also, make sure you're registered with the major airlines to receive emails about current specials before they hit the press. It will give you a much better deal on your flights and a much better chance of securing the flights you're after, because you'll have the opportunity to get in early. You just can't beat those $59 one-way deals to capital cities that are sometims offered by the airlines.

Bargain buys: best travel sites

The websites that follow offer discounted room rates, but you must book with them two to four weeks out from your holiday to obtain

Bargain buys (cont'd): best travel sites

the best deal. These wholesalers book rooms in bulk, which allows them to offer significant discounts.

- <www.hotelclub.com.au>
- <www.lastminute.com.au>
- <www.needitnow.com.au>
- <www.octopustravel.com>
- <www.wotif.com>.

Currency conversion

If you're planning a trip overseas and looking to convert your Australian dollars into foreign currency, compare the fees and charges of doing so, so you're not left out of pocket. For example, let's say that you need to convert $2000 of Australian currency into US dollars. You'll pay 1 per cent commission if you exchange the money at an Australian bank or a foreign exchange bureau. This means you'll pay $20 on top of your $2000 for the exchange. On the other hand, if you purchase American Express travellers' cheques, then you'll pay 1.1 per cent commission — costing you $22.

Although using ATM cards overseas is useful ... you will be hit with a fee of $4 or $5 every time you withdraw from an overseas ATM

Finally, although using ATM cards overseas is useful because it means you don't have to carry around a lot of money, you will be hit with a fee of $4 or $5 every time you withdraw from an overseas ATM. If you make small withdrawals, say, five withdrawals of $400, then you'll be up for a charge of $25 (if there's a $5 fee for each withdrawal).

You will also be charged a currency-conversion fee of up to 2.5 per cent—leaving you another $50 out of pocket. Therefore, the total you'll be charged for withdrawing $2000 in five lots will be $75.

The bottom line here is that you'll save $45 if you take the cash in foreign currency rather than withdrawing as you go.

Remember, that $45 may pay for a souvenir or, even better, a pair of great sandals (buying shoes overseas is much more affordable than buying them here).

Ponder point

I recently read a report stating that Australia is the third-hardest working nation in the world. Although this may sound impressive, I'm not sure it's something to be proud of.

I feel that by working hard, we miss out on taking time for ourselves and our families.

As the saying goes, the world is your oyster. From today, why not schedule in your diary some time away with your family or friends, or just on your own?

Treat yourself

One of the biggest rewards you can give yourself is to plan time away. Why not try escaping for a while? You could:

- *spend a weekend at a health spa or retreat.*
- *have a beach holiday.* Your only luggage should be a pile of trashy magazines and a good book.
- *go on a gourmet weekend.* Most of the wine regions across Australia offer the best food and wine experiences.
- *escape with the kids.* A good and very affordable place to take them away to is farm-stay accommodation (visit <www.farmstayaustralia.com.au> or <www.australianfarmtourism.com.au>).
- *take a drive out to the beach or ocean.* There is nothing as calming as spending the day by the water. Lie on the beach with your favourite magazines, as if you're on a holiday.
- *go on a picnic with your family or a group of girlfriends.* Enjoy a glass of riesling under a tree or lie on the grass and watch the clouds roll by. Ah, there is nothing more relaxing than doing this.

Chapter 5

Around your home

It's important to make your home a haven — a place where you can unwind. Some of the suggestions in this chapter will help you find a space where you can just sit and enjoy your surroundings or even soak luxuriously in a long bath

The upkeep of a family home is relentless — from paying bills to keeping the fridge stocked and the cupboards full. This no doubt takes time and money, but there are ways to save. Each of the tips in this chapter requires only a little effort to implement, but all the savings are real and ongoing.

Saving energy and water

Most people know that cutting back on their energy and water use around the home is a great way to help the environment, but many don't know what a huge difference it can make to their finances. From buying energy-efficient appliances to keeping a bucket in the shower for water run-off, there are things you can do to significantly reduce your water and energy expenses.

Before you install a rain-water tank, ensure it complies with local council regulations on tank sizes

As you read this section, try to identify the energy- and water-saving practices you could easily implement in your home. You may like to consider involving the kids in the process. You will be surprised at the ideas they'll come up with for reducing your household's footprint on the environment.

Water

Did you know that in one year the average Australian household will use enough water to fill 1000 baths? Now that water restrictions have become a way of life, there are a number of ways you can save water, such as by installing a rain-water tank.

Rain-water tanks are a great way to store water, and in most cases you will receive a rebate once you put one in. Even schools benefit from this scheme: Sydney Water offers schools that install rain-water tanks rebates of up to $2500.

Before you install a rain-water tank, ensure it complies with local council regulations on tank sizes. The rebate you can expect to receive is based on the size of your tank. As a guide, the current rebates in New South Wales are:

- $150 for a tank that holds 2000 to 3999 litres
- $400 for a tank that holds 4000 to 6999 litres
- $500 for a tank that holds 7000 litres or more.

If you connect your tank to your washing machine and toilet, expect an extra rebate of $500. Visit <www.savewater.com.au> for more on this rebate and others.

You should also make the switch to water-efficient shower heads because you'll save about $150 a year. You really won't notice the difference in your shower, but your budget will. Plus, although a simple tactic, taking shorter showers will cut your costs too. See my sister Rhonda's story, below, about her experience with water-saving devices.

Mum to mum

When water-saving devices were first introduced, our local water supplier offered to install the [water-saving] shower heads for free.

I took up the offer, and I'm glad I did because I'm saving $150 a year. Plus, there is absolutely no difference between the water-saving shower head and my old shower head, and it's saving water.

Rhonda, mother of one

Keeping your home water-efficient doesn't have to be the job of one person, namely, Mum. Get the whole family involved, as Kristen does. Read her story below.

Mum to mum

My family are all getting very au fait *with bucketing water from our showers and baths ... our washing machine water goes on the lawn — my lawn has never looked better. We use the water for our compost too. The kids love growing vegies; it is a nice activity to do with them. They love going out to water the vegie patch.*

Kristen, mother of two

Splash out with bath time

Now that you have saved water in other areas, it's time to splash out on yourself and take a long hot bath! Aim for a couple a month.

I've started implementing this myself. However, after my bath I siphon the water straight into my washing machine, which is conveniently located in my bathroom. That way, I don't feel guilty about using too much water. Thankfully, many people around Australia are doing the same due to water-use restrictions. Use the leftover water for your garden if it is easier for you.

So when was the last time you took a long hot bath? It was probably a long time ago. Like many mums, you are likely to simply hop in the shower for a quick wash and hop out before the kids start demanding your attention. However, when I visited a single friend of mine recently, I couldn't help noticing her bathroom. The room was set up like a shrine — with candles and calming oils, and sweet-smelling flowers sprinkled over the vanity and bath. It looked like an oasis in her home. I guessed that bath time for her was a well-earned ritual at the end of her day. I compared this to my very functional bathroom, which is filled with bath toys, and kids' clothes and towels that always end up on the floor — not a relaxing environment. If you feel it's time to make your bathroom a shrine, put the toys away, light some candles and enjoy a well-deserved soak!

Energy

There are many ways you can reduce your energy use around the home. One of the easiest methods of minimising your winter heating costs is to ensure your house is properly insulated, as Rhonda did:

Mum to mum

Before we moved into our unit, we installed insulation to save on heating and cooling. I believe we saved around $60 a year just by doing this. I also block all drafts to prevent heat loss, and I open the blinds whenever the sun is out to let the heat in.

Rhonda, mother of one

There are many small things you can do in your home that will cut your energy use. Simply by blocking all air drafts, as Rhonda does, you will prevent heat loss, saving you money. On the flipside, you can open your drapes when it's sunny outside to let the heat in.

Top tip: using less heating and air conditioning

If your heating costs are high, know that you can save as much as $160 a year just by reducing your heater's thermostat temperature by one degree. Also, don't forget the energy benefits of using a good old-fashioned fan instead of air conditioning in summer!

By getting kids on the energy-saving bandwagon, you can work as a team with a goal in sight. Try prompting your children to change their energy use in small ways to begin with, such as encouraging them to throw on a jumper instead of turning up the heat. Busy mum Kristen does just this, as shown in the following story:

Mum to mum

I learned to just heat the areas that I need. My kids are always wandering around in winter complaining of being cold, but they wear almost nothing — often leotards. So I'm encouraging them to put more clothes on rather than turning the heat on. I also use nice throw blankets on the couch to keep warm at night, instead of turning up the heating.

Kristen, mother of two

Finally, in tiny ways try to use less power around the house. For example, sweep the wood floors instead of vacuuming, hang the washing out instead of using a clothes dryer, and only heat and light the rooms you are using.

Ponder point

Running a family, as any mother will confess, is definitely a finely tuned balancing act. Finding the time to treat yourself can be difficult because there is always a never-ending list of jobs to do. It's understandable that you feel you can't sit down and put your feet up in front of the TV or bury yourself in a good book until everything is done.

Yet sometimes you just need to let go of the to-do list and clear your schedule. It feels amazing when you do, because when you come back to your list, it won't seem as unwieldy. So learn to diarise some time for yourself, and enlist support — be it a babysitter, partner, family member or friend — to look after the kids so you can take that break. Sadly, your list will still be there when you come back, but you'll be more refreshed and no doubt attack it with more gusto than before.

Turn-off mode

Have you noticed how many devices you leave on standby mode? They probably include computers, TVs and games consoles — the list is endless. Yet just by turning off all the appliances in your home, you can save up to $80 a year. Take a look at Diane's story, overleaf, for advice.

Mum to mum

I make sure all lights, computers, stereos and TVs are off if they're not being used. They say it doesn't cost much [to leave things on]; however, I know I can save $50 to $100 per quarter as long as I'm home to nag the kids.

Diane, mother of two

Washing

One of the most obvious ways to save energy and water is to do a full load every time you wash your clothes. Also, it's worth noting that if you wash your clothes in cold water rather than hot water, you'll save $52 a year. Bear in mind that water charges in New South Wales are expected to increase by up to 33 per cent over the next three years, and the other states are sure to follow. So change your water habits to save as much as possible

You won't be surprised to learn that the average family spends between $60 and $120 on washing powder a year. However, most large retailers sell ten-kilogram boxes of top-brand washing powders for under $50. Try to find one of these retailers, and buy your powder in bulk there.

I spent $39.99 on a ten-kilogram box of OMO, and it lasted almost a year. If you break down the costs, that's only $4.00 a kilogram. So if you compare buying ten kilograms of washing powder for $39.99 with spending $120.00 on powder over a year, you'll see that buying in bulk could save you $80.00.

Energy-efficiency star ratings

When you need to buy whitegoods, check out the items' energy-efficiency star ratings. These ratings are set by the federal government and provide you with a guide to the energy efficiency of most whitegoods and appliances. For more on this, go to <www.energyrating.gov.au>. By being energy-efficient, you will significantly reduce your costs. For instance, an energy-efficient fridge costs only 33 cents a day to run (see the top tip overleaf for more on this).

So next time you're shopping for a washing machine, choose one with a high energy- or water-efficiency rating. When you purchase machines with a four-star rating or an AAAA water-efficiency rating, you can expect to receive a rebate of $150. Remember to take note of the serial number and keep your purchase receipt to take advantage of this. Visit your water utility provider and check with your whitegoods retailer to ensure you're eligible for a rebate.

Let's just add these little water- and energy-saving gems together to see how much you'd save if you used them:

Using a water-efficient shower head	$150
Using less air conditioning	$160
Not using standby mode	$80
Washing in cold water	$52
Buying washing powder in bulk	$80
Total savings over a year	$522

It's amazing how the savings start to grow. Consider what you could do with them every year.

Top tip: money going down the drain

Your family may be like the many families across Australia that have a spare fridge sitting out in the garage. If this sounds like your brood, check how energy-efficient that old fridge is. According to an Energex Australia report, an old fridge that continually frosts over could cost you as much as $2.50 a day to run. Let's do the maths to see the savings you could make over a year:

Running an energy-wasting fridge	$912.50 ($2.50 × 365)
Running an energy-efficient fridge	$120.45 ($0.33 × 365)
Savings over a year	$792.05

To make savings to the tune of $800, it may be time for you to upgrade to a newer model. While you're doing that, buy what every mum needs — an energy-efficient dishwasher!

One woman's trash is another woman's treasure

It's unfortunate but true that we live in a throw-away society. Just take a look around your local streets, and you'll find plenty of unwanted furniture and electricals on nature strips and footpaths. Sometimes I'm amazed at what people will throw out. I've seen lounge chairs, computer tables and monitors, and beds left out on the streets. A few years ago, I picked up a fully functional TV on the side of the road — and it still works today. I even worked with someone who furnished her home almost entirely from discarded items she found in her neighbourhood streets.

You can pick up some seriously interesting furniture just by keeping an eye out

My point here is that you can pick up some seriously interesting furniture just by keeping an eye out. Of course, if you know when your local council's next clean-up day is, look out for items that could save you a few dollars then. People are usually only too happy to have their unwanted items put to use. It's a great way to recycle — saving you money and saving the planet.

Phones

Monthly phone charges are one of the ongoing costs in most families. In between your land line, your mobile and your children's mobiles (depending on their ages), the costs sure do add up. This chapter includes some ways you can make the most of your phone calls.

A phone for your needs

Phones today come with so many bells and whistles that it can be hard to get your head around the simplest of tasks. If you only need a mobile phone to make and receive calls, and for text messaging, then choose a phone that is limited to those functions. Don't pay hundreds for a new phone that has more features than you'll ever use. Shop around — don't buy the first phone you see.

When is comes to choosing a service provider that suits your requirements, consider going for one that offers free talk time between people on the same network. It is the best way to go if you have a number of phones within your family that all use the same network — as shown by Kelly in the story below.

Mum to mum

My phone provider was offering packages to customers, and one was free calls to frequently called numbers. My partner and I now call each other on our mobile phones. We can make these calls for free as long as they are preregistered. My home phone bill has dropped heaps — by at least $30 per month.

Kelly, mother of two

Saving $30 a month is great — multiply that figure by twelve months, and it makes a total saving of $360 over a year.

Capped and prepaid plans

If you have a hard time keeping your mobile phone calls under control, consider signing up for a prepaid phone plan. That way, you will be forced to stop making calls once your prepaid card hits its limit.

On the other hand, capped plans are the only way to go if you have to make lots of calls. Mind you, be wary of any phone deals offering 'free' or 'cheap' mobile phones; the cost of the handset may exceed the monthly cost of the contract.

Remember, your phone contract is a legally binding document, so read the fine print carefully to understand the terms. This is particularly important when you wish to cancel your contract, because you could be up for a hefty cost.

Messaging

When you retrieve or leave a voicemail message, it costs between 8 and 15 cents each time. As such, delete messages once you have heard them, so you won't be charged for listening to them again.

Did you know that if you send five text messages a day, it can add almost $40 to your average monthly bill? If you look at that expense over a year, sending messages can cost you an extra $480 per annum. Every text message you send costs, so work out exactly how many messages you can afford to send every day.

Top tip: paying phone bills

Make sure you pay your phone bill on time. Some phone-service providers will penalise you as much as $10 for a late payment. Even worse, if you forget to pay your bill altogether, you could be up for a reconnection fee of $50.

Combining service providers

Combining your phone, payTV and internet services can be a good way to receive discounts and rewards. For example, to make sure I was making the most of my phone, internet and payTV plans, I rang my provider; because I have these services with the one provider,

I managed to receive 125 free local calls each month — saving me about $22.

Flexibility

You should also check whether you have flexibility with your services because it may save you some cash. For example, I have an unlimited internet plan that I pay $66 a month for, but I am allowed to bring this rate down to $29.95 when I know I'm going to have a month with few downloads or I'm going to be away. Likewise, my payTV plan is flexible in that I can choose to suspend it for three months of the year. I have done this a few times, and I saved $120 as a result.

Saving on bills and groceries

Groceries are one of the biggest ongoing expenses in any household. With two growing boys who have bottomless pits for stomachs, I feel as though I'm continually topping up our household supplies. I've learned to do one major grocery shop every two weeks. I buy in bulk; I find this is the best way to keep my grocery bills down — as does Marta (see her story in the box below).

Mum to mum

I make it a priority to buy items on sale, particularly when I go grocery shopping. Most of the meat in my freezer are specials. I buy in bulk: if chicken's on sale, I'll buy five packets and freeze them. I even buy items that are close to their use-by dates because they are always discounted. People worry that they will go off too soon, but it has never happened to us, and I buy a lot. I reckon I save hundreds of dollars a year just by buying things on special.

Marta, mother of four

Try, if possible, to limit the number of times you visit the grocery store, particularly if you're the type who walks into a shop for some milk and then walks out having spent $50. I used to do this; every time I needed to get milk I'd pick up other items as well — items I wouldn't have bought if I hadn't needed milk. So be disciplined when you shop. Writing a list is one way to do this because it means you'll be more likely to buy only what you need.

Be disciplined when you shop

Take a look as some of the saving ideas below.

ALDI! ALDI! ALDI! Oi! Oi! Oi!

When it comes to the best discounted groceries, the winner is ALDI. Yes, many are now converted to this European chain of cheap grocery stores.

There is no arguing over the savings here. In fact, ALDI stands for ALbrecht DIscount. ALDI has 150 stores operating across New South Wales, the ACT, Queensland and Victoria. Nicky is one mum who values ALDI's prices. See her story overleaf.

Mum to mum

We used to spend about $350 a fortnight [on groceries]. Now we spend only about $250 on groceries. The biggest savings are made on ALDI's soy milk, breakfast cereals, organic yoghurt, dry goods and nappies.

We're shocking savers, but since I discovered ALDI supermarkets, I reckon I have saved $100 per week, which is amazing really.

Nicky, mother of one

Diane is another mum who extols the virtues of ALDI. Read about her experience with the store in the box below.

Mum to mum

I find that ALDI stores are the cheapest, and, of course, I buy in bulk when specials are on. Shopping at ALDI cuts my grocery bill by 40 per cent compared with the bill I get from Coles and Woolworths. I never buy at IGA or small independents.

Another thing I do is I buy fresh groceries daily, and the meat and vegetables on special for the day for dinner that night. I also look at what leftovers I can use and prepare my meals around them so that I don't waste food.

Diane, mother of two

Coupons and catalogues

I know it seems trite, but by taking advantage of supermarket specials, you really can save. So check the catalogues you receive from supermarkets and in the mail — like Sonia does (see below).

Mum to mum

I never used to take any notice of catalogues that came in the mail; I'd just throw them out. It was my mother-in-law who pointed out to me that you can find some great sales by scanning them. After my son was born and I had to cut back on our spending, I started checking out the catalogues that arrived. I found that the weekly specials left us with significant savings.

Sonia, mother of one

You should also look for coupons and vouchers that will cut your grocery costs. The first coupon ever was issued by Coca-Cola back in 1894. The company offered one coupon for a free glass of Coke. Since then, vouchers have become widely used across the world. (In America alone, 86 per cent of people use them!) Australians are starting to use them more here, particularly the discounted petrol vouchers available from some stores.

You'll find heaps of coupons on the back of grocery receipts, often called Shop-A-Dockets. You'll find discounts on local restaurants, video hire, and other products and services. I recently found one that offered 15 per cent off school shoes and another one that offered two free doughnuts. Because I was shopping with my youngest son at the time, I took advantage of it! The only disadvantage is that they expire really quickly, so you need to be quick about taking up the special offers. Read about how Kelly saves using Shop-A-Dockets below.

Mum to mum

My local video store always advertises on Shop-A-Dockets, and I almost never pay more than $4 for a new-release video or DVD as a result. Sometimes I can even have these for three days. These Shop-A-Dockets are a godsend when the kids are sick or the school holidays are on and I need something to occupy them.

We get a video at least once a fortnight. So that's a somewhat decent saving over a year. And when we sit down to watch a movie together, we make our own treats to eat in front of the TV, rather than buying food from the video store.

Kelly, mother of two

Also, don't discard any pizza vouchers that arrive in your letterbox. I decided to take advantage of one of the vouchers offered by Domino's Pizza. The price the company offered for a medium-sized pizza seemed exceptionally cheap, so I took my voucher along and paid only $6.99. In the past I would normally have paid $11.99. It was a great saving, and for such a low price, the pizza was worth a night off from cooking.

Online savings

As you know, shopping online has many benefits. It saves you not only money but also time. It's worth checking the deals online — you'll find everything from arts and crafts to electronics, toys and homewares. However, before you buy through any website, make sure that the site is secure, and that you've read its terms and conditions. Browse these sites:

- <*www.buckscoop.com.au*>. Buckscoop is an online directory that links you to hundreds of websites offering product discounts. You'll find sites for everything you can imagine, from the home and the office to the outdoors.
- <*www.dealsdirect.com.au*>. This website offers all the items available at large department stores. It has plenty of bargains — and discounts of over 30 per cent on a number of leading products.
- <*www.graysonline.com.au*>. If you are after some cheap wines, watch out for the online wine auctions at this site.
- <*www.oo.com.au*>. This company provides you with another place you can grab a bargain. You'll find plenty of name brands and quality products at clearance prices — and savings of up to 80 per cent off retail prices. The company has agreements and relationships with many leading factories, distributors and retailers around the world. These agreements allow it to buy overstock at significant discounts, which it then passes on to customers. There is nothing this site does not offer.

Jingle bells, jingle bills

There are many ways you can save money on Christmas events and gifts. You could try being creative, as Rachelle does (read her story below).

Mum to mum

I always use the kids' paintings as wrapping paper. My daughter brings home about five paintings on butcher paper a week. Last year I bought a huge roll of butcher paper from IKEA, stamps and paint. My kids had a ball painting them in red and green for a few afternoons. My back-up plan is the two-dollar shop, where I stock up on wrapping paper and ribbon. It is so cheap, but it still makes presents look lovely, particularly if you use heaps of ribbon.

Rachelle, mother of two

Another way you can save is to plan ahead. Set a budget and ask yourself, 'How much can I afford to spend on gifts?' Before you even take one step into a shopping centre, make a list of the people you wish to buy gifts for. Alongside each name, put down a cash limit for the person's gift.

Top tip: transferring to a credit card with a lower interest rate

It makes sense to transfer to a low–interest rate credit card before the Christmas rush. It's worth putting in some time checking out your credit card options. Bear in mind that if you transfer your balance to a new card, you'll need to make sure your old credit card provider processes the final repayment on your new card; otherwise you'll pay interest on the same debt on both cards until the first one is paid off.

Also, where possible, try to pay later. If you use your credit card constantly, then it makes sense to use lay-by for some of your costly purchases, particularly if you see something in the months prior to Christmas. Making small monthly repayments on lay-by can help you keep your credit card bills under control.

Kris Kringle

Shopping for Christmas gifts for everyone can be exhausting, not to mention expensive. One way to alleviate the pressure to buy gifts for everyone on Christmas day is to apply the Kris Kringle approach. This works wonders for large families, or even groups of friends, if you're hosting Christmas dinner. Firstly, have everyone put his or her name in a hat. Secondly, ask each person to draw a name out of the hat. The name everyone picks will be the name of whomever he or she has to buy for. This way, everyone receives a gift. Set a budget that everyone has to stick to — say, $25 to $30. This will save you money and time, because you'll be buying for only one person. At family Christmas functions, you may like to rig the Kris Kringle so that the kids receive presents from all the adults.

If you can't gather everyone together before Christmas to draw names, then, as the host, nominate who buys for whom.

Hiring help around the home

For any mum who is working full time and finding it difficult to keep the family home clean, a cleaner is a necessity. After all, when you're working hard and don't have older children or a partner to help you with cleaning, you will need some help. Hiring a cleaner will save you time and energy — leaving you with the opportunity to do the things you enjoy. Use your weekends to spend time with your family or entertain your friends.

If you're worried about spending the money, remember that you don't need to have a cleaner in every week — you could schedule one in for every two or three weeks, or even once a month. Kristen (read her story below) is a mum who knows the benefits of hiring help.

Mum to mum

I get my home cleaned every fortnight. It's definitely my treat — I love coming home every second Tuesday.

Kristen, mother of two

A live-in helper was just the answer for Diane. Read her story in the box below.

Mum to mum

Recently I put an ad in the paper for live-in help. I now have a Romanian lady who is the same age as I am, and who is lovely and unbelievable around the house. She is like an angel.

She has totally landscaped my gardens and supplied all the plants at no charge. I now have a vegie garden. She has recovered all my dining chairs for $2 per chair, and fixed my lounge suite and a million other things. My house is totally spotless and looks fantastic. I pay her $200 a week… she does the shopping, picks the kids up and cooks.

For any woman on her own, it's worth having a live-in housekeeper, particularly if she is working full time. That way you can stay sane, get out and about, and have more time to work — providing you with extra income to cover the costs of a housekeeper. This is much more satisfying than unrewarding housework. It is the ultimate spoil. Forget about a day spa; for the same money, I'd rather have all my housework done — and I mean all my housework. If your home is spotless, your head will be clearer and life will be much more blissful. The only downside is that it can be invasive to have someone in your home. So you have to make sure you weigh that up. For me, it works. I have cut many corners in order to keep her, but she is fabulous.

Diane, mother of two

Lynelle runs an event business and regularly travels interstate each month. She outsources all the cleaning and makes sure she treats herself in between. Read her story below.

Mum to mum

I make sure I outsource everything, and I do not believe caring for myself is a luxury. It is my way of life and should be everyone's if [you] wish to stay sane.

Mum to mum (cont'd)

I've been a single mother of two for the past ten years and could not have achieved success in my business without taking this course of action.

My cleaner, gardener, massage therapist, hairdresser, car cleaner and all the other professionals I use in my life save me... heaps of time. My hourly rate at my work is $250, and my average spend on services is $40 an hour.

Lynelle, mother of two

Asking the kids to help

During my career, I have required the help of cleaners. At times, however, depending on my job, I have not been able to afford a cleaner. Because my two sons are now older, when I can't afford a cleaner I give them tasks around the home. One child will vacuum the floors, and the other will wipe down surfaces. I give them $5 for each job completed, which is much cheaper than hiring a cleaner. I set aside one hour on the weekend, and we do the cleaning together then. They are quite happy to help—knowing that they're getting paid for their efforts. It also teaches them that I value what they do.

Top tip: helping at dinner time

If your kids are old enough, encourage them to start making dinner one night a week. Kids are always asking when dinner will be ready and what's for dinner. So hand them the responsibility of making dinner for the family every now and then. They may enjoy it. Remember to let them know you appreciate their help. You may just have another Jamie Oliver or Nigella Lawson in the making!

Entertaining

Spending on entertainment is usually one of the first places mums try to cut costs. However, taking time out to meet with friends and family is just as important as finding me time. Whether you like to go out to restaurants or whip up a three-course meal for your mates at home, there are ways you can entertain without it costing the earth.

Top tip: prioritising

Prioritise what is important in your to-do list each day. I prefer to do the tasks that take the most time or that are more difficult first thing in the day. Once you have completed the most important tasks for the day, it frees up your mind to finish your other jobs. It really helps to stay focused on the task you're doing. You may need to block some time out to give it your full attention. This could include not taking phone calls or emails until you are ready to tackle them.

Home entertaining

There is a lot to be said for entertaining at home. Most importantly, you don't have to worry about finding a babysitter, as long as the kids are well behaved! The other advantage is that you'll know what you're going to be served, and, if you share the load with your guests, it's a great way to unwind, save money and spend time with friends. Diane is someone who enjoys the benefits of entertaining at home. Read her experience here:

Mum to mum

I like to entertain, but I know it can be costly. I find my friends are more than happy to bring something along for dinner. If you have your guests bring something, even if it's small, it will cost you next to nothing to entertain... I really enjoy taking time out to have a meal with my friends at home.

I've always been big on entertaining (I just love doing it), but since my divorce I do have to be careful with my spending. In the past I would never have dreamed of asking people to bring something, but I do now, and people usually offer anyway... It's a lot less work for me and it works brilliantly.

Diane, mother of two

Like Diane, Carol also likes to entertain at home. She finds that hosting brunches is cheaper for her. Read her story below.

Mum to mum

One thing I love doing in home entertainment is hosting brunches. Somehow it is cheaper than making an evening meal for everyone, and it also doesn't feel like you spend all day preparing and cleaning. A chicken and champagne brunch goes down a treat!

Carol, mother of one

BYO restaurants

We all love a great night out with friends. If you're worried about the bill though, choose a BYO restaurant. Otherwise the cost of drinks alone can well exceed the cost of the food, particularly when you're out with a large group. Read *The Age Cheap Eats* guide to find out where you can dine out for cheap. Best of all, the book will help you discover new and interesting places to try with your friends.

Alcohol

Australian wines have come a long way from the 'cardboard box' varieties of the 1980s. It's really worth checking out the cleanskin wines most bottle shops sell. You'll be able to buy some really good wines for prices as low as $3.99 a bottle or buy by the dozen to receive a discount. Gone are the days when cleanskins were cheap and nasty, but if you can't stomach them, there are plenty of nice wines for under $10 per bottle.

It's really worth checking out the cleanskin wines most bottle shops sell

Remember, there's no need to pay more than $10 for a good bottle of wine. As you know, Grays Online regularly auctions cases of wines. You'll find that most times you'll pay no more than $6 or $7 a bottle if you buy a case from the site.

Take a look at Diane's experience with cleanskins in the box set out below.

Mum to mum

I'm a complete advocate of cleanskin wines. A friend put me onto the idea, and I've never looked back because the savings are significant. I'm saving about $8 a bottle now. One thing I have found is that I prefer to buy Australian cleanskins. Sometimes the international brands can be a little bitter.

Diane, mother of two

My partner generally walks in the door after work at about 6.30. Often the dinner is going, the kids are whining for food, the bath is running, the dogs are desperate for a bone and several baskets of washing are sitting in corners of the house in various stages of completion. It's hell in there, and there is still so much more to be done in that hour so that I can get the kids into bed by 7.30 and put my feet up with my partner.

So I corral him the minute he steps over the threshold and give him a series of jobs. There are often so many tasks that he doesn't know where to start. Yet we can usually get through it and snatch a moment of peace by 7.30. So what's my point? Well sometimes that hard-earned reward you've been saving for would be better spent on your partner.

Families are all about balance, and sometimes the best reward for you may be having some time to yourself while your partner goes on a golf day with friends or a boys' night out at the pub. Hopefully your partner is a great tower of strength for you, but sometimes you need to keep his batteries charged too. That way, next time there is some time in his schedule, you can give him the kids, and go treat yourself.

Treat yourself

If you want to pamper yourself, try the following pick-me-ups:

- *Freshen up your bedroom.* If your bedroom is looking a bit tired, some rearranging could bring it back to life. Buying new pillow slips, cushions and scented candles, and removing any excess clutter, does magic. Make your room a place to restore your energy and revitalise yourself.
- *Hold a charity event in your home.* You may like to stage a 'girls' night in' event and raise money for your favourite charity or cause. Gather your girlfriends together, and ask everyone to bring a plate and a donation. These types of events can be held at any time; they don't have to take place in the evening — you can hold a breakfast if that's easier. There is nothing more rewarding than giving to a worthy cause.
- *Indulge in some exotic teas and chocolates.* Ask your friends over and try some of the delicious products on the market.
- *Brighten up a wall with a painting or print you've been eyeing.* Or, even better, get creative and take a drawing or painting course.

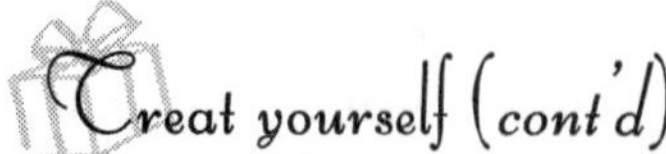

Treat yourself (cont'd)

- *Make your garden or courtyard an area you can escape to.* A lot of people get a kick out of tending to their garden and simply enjoying some time outside. Replace broken pots or freshen up your sanctuary with some plants.
- *Plant fresh herbs or even grow a veggie patch.* There's nothing like having freshly grown ingredients at home. Also, kids enjoy helping with the gardening — so put them in charge of watering the plants.

Chapter 6

Teaching the children

As parents, from the moment our children are born, right through to when they take their very first job, we fork out money to ensure they receive the best possible start in life. You may find it hard to imagine cutting costs on your children, but you can do it without scrimping on the things you believe are important for them.

Use this chapter to find ways to cut back on your children's expenses and save. The savings tactics you'll learn will bring you instant financial rewards—allowing you to have some money to treat yourself with, and perhaps the kids and your significant other.

This chapter also focuses on the importance of teaching your children the value of money. Whenever I give talks, the same question invariably comes up: 'How can I teach my children about money?' Well let me show you how you can give your children good financial sense. For many parents who feel they're not good at managing money, this can be a struggle. But I guarantee that teaching your children to understand their finances will reward not only them but also you.

If you give your kids the best financial education, it will provide them with a gift for life

Your children's perspective on money will inform their attitude to money management as adults. This means you may not see the immediate effects of teaching them the value of money, but you will in the long run.

After all, wouldn't it be great to know that your children will grow up having the confidence to manage their money without constantly asking you for handouts?

Ponder point

'Take care of the luxuries, and the necessities will take care of themselves.'

Dorothy Parker

Financial rewards for life

If you give your kids the best financial education, it will provide them with a gift for life. As a parent, I know that in today's society it's definitely a challenge for parents to educate children about money. Today's children are growing up in a world where money pops out of ATMs as if by magic and can be transferred over the phone or the web, and where payments can be made using plastic cards.

In this virtual world of money exchange, it can be hard for children to comprehend where money comes from, how it can be saved and how people can afford to spend it. To illustrate this further, when my oldest son was three years old, he asked me to buy him a toy. I refused and said I had no money, yet every time we passed an ATM he would run up to the machine and demand that I take money out of it. He just thought that anyone could get money from a big hole in the wall—try explaining the intricacies of ATMs to a three year old!

It is easy to see how many children grow up not understanding how to save and manage their money. The scary thing is that most will obtain credit cards before knowing how to control their money. This is clear from the following quote from Katherine:

Mum to mum

My nephew, who is eighteen and works part time, has just had a credit card approved with an $18 000 limit. For a young person with no financial skills, this is a recipe for disaster.

Katherine, mother of two

I share Katherine's view. Perhaps this explains why bankruptcy rates for people under 30 have increased substantially over the past few years.

It's important to teach your kids the value of money. By you doing so, it will enable them to make wise decisions with their earnings in the future. The tips in this chapter show you how essential it is to give your kids responsibility for their money, savings and buying decisions.

Talking to your children about money

Get into the habit of talking to your children about money — the earlier, the better. Anna is one mum who sticks to this — read her story below.

Mum to mum

I'm a single parent, and I have included my daughter in conversations about money. I even show her my bank statements and explain the various items on them. She is now twelve and wants a mobile phone. I give her $10 a week. I tell her that if she can save half of the phone's cost, I will pay for the other half.

The phone she wants is fairly basic (I can get it for $80 on eBay). She has a few weeks to save for it and has a put a jar aside that is labelled 'mobile phone'.

When she reaches the $40 savings mark, I will give her $40 for the phone. I want her to understand what it means to save for something, and doing this helps her understand how to budget.

Anna, mother of one

As I mentioned earlier, ATMs have led children to believe there is an endless supply of money. Credit cards don't help either. Because children don't see cash being exchanged in transactions, they develop a distorted perception of value. So begin with something as simple as explaining the cost of a grocery item and how all your grocery costs add up on your food bill.

By the same token, involve your children in some of your money-making decisions; of course, you should take their ages into account when doing this.

Accountability and responsibility

Give your children responsibility for what they spend. Rather than just buying them things as they ask for them, give your kids a set amount of cash to spend — and don't give in when they ask for more. For example, if your children are at a school fete and you give them $10 to spend while there, they will actually think about whether they need an item before they buy it. Your money will last much longer. Take a leaf out of Robyn's book. Her story is below.

Mum to mum

We give our daughter a weekly allowance. She can spend it on anything she likes, but once she has spent all the money given to her, she has to wait to receive more. I believe this fosters good discipline — helping her to learn that she has to earn money and wait until she has enough of it before she can spend it. It took a while for her to grasp the idea, but we stuck to our guns. Sometimes she spends more than her allowance. When she does, I tell her

Mum to mum (cont'd)

that I will give her the money, but that it will have to come out of the following week's allowance.

Robyn, mother of two

Give your children pocket money, but help them to work out the difference between saving and spending money. Read Lana's story, below, for an illustration.

Mum to mum

We give my son a monthly allowance, and he pays for everything except anything to do with school (he is in year 8). He buys presents for the family, and pays for all his internet-game charges, books (for leisure) and movie tickets. Any money he has left over at the end of the year is his. This has taught him to value money and save when he needs something. It's important that he understands the concept of delaying gratification, and deciding what he really wants and needs.

Lana, mother of one

If you have teenage children, help them set a monthly budget; it doesn't have to be strict — just show them the basics. For example, help them understand that they need to allocate a certain amount of cash from their allowance for clothing and entertainment.

Teach your children to shop around for the item they want. My son searches on Google to see which store is offering the best price for the item he wants. He also scours through specials in catalogues. He understands that prices vary from store to store and that he can save by finding the best deal.

Saving

Encourage your children to save by rewarding them when they do. For example, if they save half the money for something they want to buy, you could reward their efforts by contributing the other half.

Children get a kick out of having their own money. Open a bank account in their name and have them put money into it. This will help them understand the basic principles of saving. If you want to start with something simpler, buy them a piggy bank, as Marion did (read her story below).

Mum to mum

My daughter was around three when she began to understood the concept of using money to buy things. We wanted her to understand the concept of saving as well. The bank was giving out these great-big, pink piggy banks. My daughter would put her money into it, and then open it up and stack the coins to see how big the pile was.

Marion, mother of one

Investment basics

Explain to your children the basics of investing. I'm not talking about showing them how to become a stockbroker—just give them the nuts and bolts of investing. You could use your house as an example. (Hopefully it has increased in value!) You could say that you bought the home for $400 000 and then explain why its value has increased over the years. During my own financial education over the past fifteen years, my children have become accustomed to learning about investing. Now they understand how the stock market works. If your kids can grasp the basics of investing while young, they will find it much easier to learn the intricacies as they grow older. Sarah's story, below, is a good example of this.

Mum to mum

I always wanted to follow my dad's example, but it took several years before I started to think seriously about investing. I was earning good money and decided to add some more blue-chip shares [to] my Coles shares.

When my daughter, Jessie, was a year old, the opportunity to start a share portfolio for her came up via an old client of mine. I'd helped him on some work, and in return he bought 150 Westpac shares for Jessie in her name.

In the meantime, I'd been saving all the money she had been given from family members in a regular savings account. When she turned three, the money accumulated in the account was quite significant.

I decided to buy some AGL and ANZ shares in Jessie's name. Whenever Westpac offered a rights issue to buy more shares, I accepted the offer and paid for them myself but kept them in her name.

Sarah, mother of one

Sarah credits her father for introducing her to shares when she was eighteen. Like her father, Sarah taught her daughter Jessie the value of investing. Sarah opted to keep all the shares in Jessie's name and pay the tax on any capital gains herself. She reinvested all dividends earned. In the case of AGL, which does not have a reinvestment plan, Sarah had all the dividends directed to Jessie's savings account. Sarah explains how this has worked out here:

Mum to mum

Jessie has an ATM card attached to her savings account so that she can access her money. These are her shares and her money. Whenever it's her father's or my birthday, she uses the money for presents. To buy any other items, such as clothes or special things (for instance, her iPod), she uses this money. We do give her pocket money, but it's very minimal.

The money gives her a sense of independence. She reads her statements regularly and keeps track of her portfolio. She says, 'One day I'll buy a car'. Now that she is seventeen, it's not that far away.

Sarah, mother of one

If you're worried about your child paying too much tax on his or her investments, you can invest in shares for him or her in your name. This means you will pay all the capital gains tax (explained in more detail in in chapter 8) on the investments at your marginal tax rate.

Finally, don't forget to teach your children the value of giving. Thankfully, most schools endorse a number of community charity events. When your kids are asked to donate a gold coin for a worthy cause at school, encourage them to give.

The investing principle

In this chapter I recommend that you teach your children how investing can make money. Apart from showing them how a home is an investment, you can also demonstrate to them how investing in shares and managed funds can generate money. Of course, before you invest in these, please seek financial advice. Below is an explanation of how these types of investments work.

Managed funds and shares

One simple and effective way to start a savings plan is to invest in a managed fund. Once you have set up the fund, it takes a lot of the guesswork out of what you can save. (There is much more on managed funds in chapter 8, Money makes money.)

One benefit of investing in managed funds (and shares) is that you can invest your money when you have it, rather than having money taken out of your pay every payday. This may suit parents who don't always have the ready cash.

As for share investing, when money becomes available, say, from gifts from relatives, it's a great time to start a share portfolio for your kids. It is important that you reinvest all dividends earned over time. Your mindset should be to 'set and forget'. To give you an example, a colleague of mine decided to do just that when her first child was born. She had been given $700 from family members. Rather than spend the money, she saw the windfall as an opportunity to start a share portfolio for her son. Having never bought shares before, but with an understanding of long-term investing, she opened an online share trading account and bought shares for her son in a leading bank. Five years down the track, she is happy with her decision and continues to steadily build a portfolio.

It is important that you reinvest all dividends earned over time

My son's managed fund

When my son Daniel was thirteen years old, he had saved $350 in his bank account. I asked him if he would like to see his money grow. Obviously, he said he would, but it would mean he would have to withdraw the money from the bank and put it into a managed fund. The fund I had in mind was one I'd been investing in for about two years, and its returns were fairly substantial — approximately 30 per cent. This was a gamble, but I felt fairly confident that the managed fund would continue to perform. It's been almost three years since my son's initial $350 investment, his contribution has grown to over $750. This has helped him understand how investing works. Plus, the return he received was certainly more than the 0.5 per cent he would have received if his money had sat in the bank.

Top tip: piggy banks

There's another reason I encourage my children to use piggy banks or even money jars to save. I credit my son's piggy bank for teaching him to add when he was in kindergarten. It really helped him with his maths. Whenever he received money from me or someone else for his birthday, he'd put the cash in his piggy bank and count it.

Kids' bank accounts

Unfortunately, most banks don't offer much in the way of children's savings accounts. Most of the time, the account fees alone eat up any earnings in these accounts. However, setting up a bank account for your children is a simple, easy way to help them save and understand investing.

You may like to open a BankWest Kids' Bonus Saver account, which offers 10 per cent interest for children under fifteen. This rate of interest is way ahead of those set by BankWest's competitors, and, best of all, the Kids' Bonus Saver is fee-free. Visit <www.bankwest.com.au> for details.

Education rewards for life

Regardless of whether you plan to send your child to a public or private school or university, educational costs will be one of your major expenses. Giving your children the best education you can afford will be something they can carry with them for the rest of their lives. Below are a few suggestions that should help you plan for their education.

Savings on education

The Australian Scholarships Group (ASG) is a not-for-profit organisation and friendly society that helps families save for the education of their children at both secondary-school and tertiary levels. The organisation offers a saving program to parents (or grandparents) that forces them to put money away in anticipation of their kids' educational expenses. Parents do this by making small, regular payments into the fund over the period their child is in the program.

The earnings on contributions in the fund are then pooled and divided among the fund's beneficiaries, and paid to your child in the form of a scholarship or independent scholarship allowance while they are undertaking study. Because the fund is designed specifically for educational expenses, it fulfils the requirements of the *Income Tax Assessment Act 1997*'s (the Tax Act's) 'scholarship plan' provisions, which provides a tax concession that allows parents to maximise their children's benefits.

Children can be enrolled any time up until the age of ten. Visit <www.asg.com.au> for more information.

Education saving plans

Education saving plans (ESP) are intended to help parents save for their child's education. They are offered by most major financial institutions, and operate like managed funds, whereby contributions are made monthly or in a lump sum. The benefit of this type of savings plan, is that it is classified as a 'scholarship plan', so it provides tax advantages that are not available with other types of saving and investment products. To see the ESPs available at the Commonwealth Bank, go to <www.commbank.com.au/educationsavings>, and to see Australian Unity's offering, go to <www.australianunity.com.au> and select the 'investments' menu.

Private schools

Part of the government's funding to private schools also includes subsidies for students who are from low-income families. This can make a big difference to your finances — as Diane's story, below, shows. Diane's daughter was accepted into a private school shortly before the family fell on hard times.

Mum to mum

Two years before my daughter was due to start high school, I put her name on the list of one of the private schools. I was really happy when she was accepted, but the only problem was paying the school fees. I had recently divorced from her father, and we were both struggling to get by.

I rang the school and told it I was having financial hardship. It told me about the government subsidy for low-income families. I had to fill out a form so that I could be means-tested. I was granted the subsidy. It was a great relief to know that this option is available, because I really wanted my daughter to go to the school.

My young son attends a Catholic school, and I was paying around $150 a week for him to go there. When I spoke to the head principal and explained my situation, the school was very understanding — now I pay $50 a week towards the fees. Once I'm back on my feet, I will pay off the yearly school fees.

Diane, mother of two

Some number crunching

So now that you are a little wiser about teaching your kids about money, and, hopefully, have a better understanding of why this will set them on the road to a solid financial future, what about the upfront costs? You can make significant savings on your kids' expenses — and you need to. Check out the facts below on how much it takes to raise a child — it may just make you think twice about what you spend on your brood.

Here's a sobering thought: a report commissioned by the National Centre for Social and Economic Modelling at Canberra University in 2003 found that the total costs of raising two children from birth to the age of 20 are $448 000, or nearly 23 per cent of the average gross household income of $1324 a week. To simplify this even further, that's a cost of about $310 a week — a staggering prospect for many parents. This figure takes into account most of the costs involved in parenting, including housing, transport, food, recreation, clothing and education.

The total costs of raising two children from birth to the age of 20 are $448 000

Ponder point

Q: *I feel as though I am doing okay, juggling so many things, but at times I feel that I'm short-changing my family or my work. What's the best way to get balance?*

A: If you're feeling like you're doing okay most of the time, then that's great, but as with most mums, trying to find the right balance is a never-ending dilemma. No matter what you're doing — whether you're at work or helping the kids — as long as you are giving it 100 per cent of your attention, then that's all you can ask of yourself. When you're with your kids, just concentrate on them — and the same goes for other jobs. It's about giving your best in the moment.

Savings from the cradle

A recent survey conducted by <www.motherinc.com.au> found that new parents tend to splurge on extravagant items, such as prams, electric toy cars and designer rocking horses. Apparently, of the new mums out there, 40 per cent spend between $1000 and $3000 on new baby items; 15 per cent, $3000 to $5000; and a few can afford to splurge out, spending between $5000 and $10 000. All this takes place in only the first few months of a baby's life!

The truth is, children will grow out of these items before you know it. Rather than buying everything new and then having to offload them in a short time, it makes sense to borrow the items you need and pass them on. If you're a first-time mum, scout around at local garage sales, second-hand stores, newspapers, such as the *Trading Post*, and eBay for baby items. Make sure that your purchases meet all the regulatory safety standards.

A second-hand cot can cost as little as $50 — the same goes for a preloved pram. Baby car seats are also very cheap second-hand; I recall selling my baby car seat for $20. So you clearly don't have to spend thousands to set up a nursery. Don't forget to call on family and friends; many people are happy to offload their baby furniture, particularly when their kids have outgrown everything and it's only taking up valuable space in their home.

A colleague of mine was due to have her third child, many years after having her second child. Because the pregnancy was a little unexpected, she had already offloaded all her baby furniture. She decided to hire a baby capsule for the first three months, but when she enquired about the cost, she was staggered to find that the cost had increased significantly. She searched on eBay and found a capsule for less than the hire price she'd been offered. After three months she decided to sell the capsule on eBay (the baby had hardly left any marks on it). She managed to sell the capsule for the same price as what she had bought it for, so it cost her nothing at all.

A bonus for baby and you

You may feel that the government's generous baby bonus justifies your reasons for spending. However, if you are a new mum and can make some savings on baby equipment, consider putting the baby bonus towards long-term financial goals for your children, such as setting up a managed fund for your kids or buying shares in their names. You may also like to set a little aside to buy a treat for you — an overworked and overtired new mum. After nine months carrying your little bundle of joy and many sleepless nights, you deserve a little treat for yourself.

It is also worth knowing that people can get Family Tax Benefits A and B from Centrelink. The benefits are means-tested. There is also an immunisation allowance available from Centrelink. Visit <www.familyassist.gov.au> for more on these benefits.

Top tip: popcorn and drink deals

When taking your kids to the movies, don't fall for the popcorn and drink deals. These are hideously expensive.

I ask my kids to buy drinks and treats from the local supermarket before the movie, and they don't mind at all — as long as they have something to munch on while they're watching the movie.

To be honest, there is a lot more variety in the supermarket than at the movie candy bar anyway. Look below so that you can compare the costs:

Popcorn and drink deal from the cinema	$10.00
A soft drink and pack of lollies from Woolworths	$2.50
Saving	$7.50

You could spend the $7.50 on a discounted kids' movie ticket or, better still, put the money towards an adult ticket for you.

Shopping for kids

There are many ways you can cut costs when shopping for your children. This section shows you how.

Bargain websites

Below is a list of websites that cater for children. The sites sell everything from toys and games to clothes and stationery.

- <*www.kidsbits.com.au*>. This website specialises in toys for toddlers. It also sells learning toys and products for mums.
- <*www.toysonline.com.au*>. Don't let your kids get their hands on this site or you'll be fighting them for the computer. It offers numerous kids' toys, regular sales and bargain-bin items at discounted prices.
- <*www.twodollars.com.au*>. This website offers hundreds of everyday items for kids. You'll find all sorts of things (not just kids' stuff), from clothing and toys to electronics and DVDs.

Sales

You just cannot go past sales for kids' clothes. I wait for the sales in the major department stores before I buy my son's clothes. Target, Kmart and Big W have huge specials at these times. You really don't have to wait long for the sales; they seem to be always on.

Top tip: looking for free stuff

The good things in life are free, so utilise whatever freebies you can find. Make use of parks and free concerts, for example.

Top tip (cont'd): looking for free stuff

Shopping centres and libraries often host free activities for children during school holidays. Also, your local paper will list free events happening in your area each week.

School shoes

School shoes are a yearly expense. If your kids are heavy on their feet, you could find yourself buying shoes every six months. A better option would be to wait for the big department-store sales, and shop for your kids' shoes then.

After having tried the cheaper school shoes, which never last for more than three months on my kids' feet, I vowed to only buy top brands in school shoes. For me, that means Clarks school shoes. With two boys who require school shoes every year, I wait for the sales at Myer or David Jones before I buy.

Wait for the big department-store sales, and shop for your kids' shoes then

I can save 30 per cent off the normal retail price when shoes are on sale. The only thing I do find is that I have to be quick to get a pair that fits. The last pair of Clarks shoes I bought cost me $59.95 on sale, which was better than the regular price of $89.95. Clarks shoes last a whole year, so buying them is effectively much cheaper than buying shoes of a lower quality, which you are more likely to have to replace often.

Bargain buys

Read the following tips on how to save:

- *Hire DVDs and videos for free from large libraries or community centres.* They usually also offer holiday activities for children to help them pass the time. Most of the time they are free or have a minimal charge, so you'll need to get in early with booking your child in.
- *See if your motoring association offers discounts on certain things.* Most of the motoring associations, such as NRMA and RACV, offer discounts to theme parks, zoos and kids' activities. Check your membership prior to purchasing tickets. I bought tickets to Warner Bros. Movie World and saved around $15 by using the discounts offered by my motoring association. Just remember to purchase them in advance of your trip.
- *Purchase yearly passes, such as zoo or theme-park memberships.* They are expensive to buy upfront, but if you go to the zoo or a theme park more than a couple of times a year, a yearly pass will be more economical. It's always nice to have this one up your sleeve, particularly in school holidays when you have to find things to do with the kids.
- *Let family members and friends know what the kids would like for Christmas or their birthday.* If your kids want money, help them to save it for something they want later down the track.

Discount chemist outlets

Discount chemists provide another area that you can cut costs in. If one of your children regularly needs medication, you can save a bundle. Sonia relates her experience of this below.

Mum to mum

When my son was under twelve months, I would go through one can of formula a week. Formula is expensive; if I bought it from Coles or Woolworths, I would pay $20 a can. I found it was far more economical to go out to a discount chemist that is about 20 minutes away from my home. I would save around $3 on a tin of baby formula at the chemist, so I would buy four cans there at a time. That alone saved me $12 a month. Plus, I would buy other things for my son while there. It was worth the trip — I saved, at the minimum, $20 on my baby expenses a month. I would try to go once a month.

Sonia, mother of one

You can see from the story above that Sonia was able to save $20 a month — giving her $240 in savings a year.

Second-hand school uniforms

Buying second-hand school uniforms is a favourite saving tip of mine. I have done it all through the schooling of both my sons. For the most part, the clothes are in good condition, and when you compare the costs of buying new clothes with buying second-hand ones, the savings are significant. By doing this, you not only recycle clothes but also contribute to a school's much-needed funds. With a preloved school shirt costing as little as $5, there is no argument as to why buying second-hand clothes is a must.

I have saved hundreds of dollars by using the second-hand clothing store at my children's school. Considering how often kids lose articles of school clothing (be they hats, sports gear or pullovers), subject them to general wear and tear, and grow out of them, this tip is a winner.

Below are just a few examples of the second-hand items I've bought. Compare the prices of those and new school clothes.

	Second-hand price	Retail price
School T-shirt	$5	$25
School shorts	$5	$20
School trousers	$12	$39
School tracksuit	$25	$100

As you can see, there are a number of big pluses with buying second-hand school clothing, including the following:

- It saves you money.
- It saves you time because there is no need to shop around (the second-hand store is usually on the school premises).
- The money you spend goes back to the school for fundraising.
- It recycles clothes.

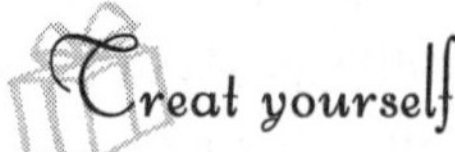

Treat yourself

Try treating you and your family in the following ways:

- *Go out for dinner one night a week, or schedule in one for every second week, and take turns at picking a restaurant.* The idea here is to give you a break so that you can spend some time with the kids rather than staying in the kitchen.
- *Start a babysitting club with other mums.* This way, you and your partner can have some together without the kids.
- *Indulge yourself and the kids in some home-made ice-cream, the really nice stuff.* Or buy the real 'creamy' gourmet brands of ice-cream. You can also indulge in some good, old-fashioned ice-cold treats from the local milk bar.
- *Schedule in one early-morning walk a week with your kids, and finish up with a coffee for you and a milkshake for them.* It's a nice way to start the day; you just need to be organised so that you can be back in time to get ready for school and work.
- *Make time for a regular facial or skin treatment for the next six months.*
- *Slot in a babysitter so that you can have a break during the day.* That way, you are not hanging out for your partner to come home and relieve you.
- *Get back to the gym or go for regular walks to regain some me time and exercise time.*

- *Stay in touch with other mums, and don't forget your friends without kids.*
- *Freshen up your wardrobe.* If you've had a baby recently, after months of wearing only maternity wear, you'll be glad to get back into some new clothes.
- *Learn an activity with your child.* You could take up drawing classes together or even learn to ride a bike together.
- *Plan a holiday that you and your kids will enjoy.* Encourage them in the decision making. If you have very young children, here's a word of advice: make sure your accommodation has babysitting (otherwise you may feel as though you haven't had a holiday at all). The best holidays I've had with my kids have been those that had plenty of entertainment, a pool on hand and activities to keep my children occupied. Kids' clubs work well for children under five, and some even offer great activities for five to twelve year olds, such as movie nights and bowling.

Chapter 7

Clothes and accessories

Have you ever watched one of those make-over transformation shows? Usually you're shown a 'before shot' and, after the make-over, an 'after shot' of the model. At the end of the show, the transformed woman is always smiling and looking fabulous. Apart from her new hairstyle and make-up, she also feels great because of her new clothes. It's amazing how good you feel once you rid yourself of your old and tired wares.

Many women fall into the trap of rising every morning and putting on the same old outfit because they don't have time to think about mixing this with that. Yet a change in your wardrobe is a great way to generate positive energy, which will give you a whole new outlook on life. Believe it or not, it really doesn't take a lot of effort to update your clothes. You can start with a subtle change; the trick is to find something that requires minimum effort but works for you. Take, for example, a friend of mine who always looks great. She swears by the simple rule of black, black and more black, but she also adds a touch of colour via an accessory, a handbag or make-up.

Declare a day of beauty

Why not declare a day of beauty for yourself? This is a great way to treat yourself before the start of a busy week. (In fact, I believe there should be a national day of beauty.) Once a month, preferably on a weekend (Sundays are best), give yourself a morning of beauty.

Why not declare a day of beauty for yourself?

Start the day with a face mask; then fill up your bathtub with bubbles and exfoliate your skin with a loofah. Afterwards, moisturise from top to toe. For the next hour, go through your wardrobe; give away clothes you no longer wear and hunt for garments suitable for the new season. You will feel cleansed not only on the outside but also on the inside.

Of course, for some mums it may be too difficult to find time for this. If that sounds like you, you may find it easier to treat yourself while juggling other things; for example, put on a face mask while making dinner, or paint your nails while watching the news in front of the TV.

Out of the closet

If your wardrobe is full of clothes yet you're constantly saying that you've got nothing to wear, it's time to declutter your wardrobe. The first step is to make some crucial decisions about what you want to give away, so that you will have space for the clothes you want to save. If an outfit is out of date or no longer fits you, give it away or donate it to a charity.

The problem with having a wardrobe full of clothes is that you can easily forget what gems are harbouring in the back. I know I've been caught out once. I thought I didn't have a pair of navy trousers, so I went out and bought one — only to find that I had some trousers hiding in the recesses of my closet.

Top tip: Clothing Can Make A Difference

Clothing Can Make A Difference (at <www.ccmad.com.au>) is an organisation set up by two remarkable women. They collect quality, preloved suits and workwear to give to women who have suffered from domestic violence. Their aim is to use clothing as a tool to help victims of abuse rebuild their self-esteem so that they can take a small step towards getting their lives back on track, such as having quality clothes to wear at job interviews.

Hanging space

Once you've cleared out your wardrobe, organise your clothes by type — that is, divide them into skirts, shirts, pants and dresses.

That way, you'll be able to see all the similar items at a glance, just as clothes are displayed in boutiques and department stores.

Take a thorough look at your accessories and jewellery, and discard any old and broken pieces. Clean and polish what you want to keep. The same goes with handbags — pull them out of the closet and wipe them over. If you find any old bags you don't like anymore — out they go. (Remember though, when you go to replenish your wardrobe, adopt an 'only buy when on sale' attitude.)

Also, great shoes complete a wardrobe, so do not neglect your feet. Comfort is important, and a great pair of shoes will carry you through the day. I don't believe in compromising when it comes to shoes; however, I do wait for the sales before I purchase a new pair.

Designer labels

There are only a handful of women who can afford the price tags designer labels carry, so it's no wonder that designer imitations have taken off in a big way. No sooner does a designer show off his or her wares, when the very next day the same outfits or accessories are on display in general retail clothing stores.

The quality of designer imitations has vastly improved — not only clothes but also jewellery and handbags. You really no longer have to pay an exorbitant price for a Gucci handbag when there are similar bags out there. So go for cheap and chic, not cheap and tacky.

In 2007, when retailer Target launched an affordable Stella McCartney range, it knew it was onto a winner. The range shifted the perception of Target as a discount retailer to a store that is in touch with the latest fashion. So before you visit an expensive boutique, visit a larger retail chain store.

Perhaps this trend is catching on across the globe — more designers are bringing their clothes to the people. American designer and dresser to the stars Vera Wang has done just that. Wang's gowns sell for thousands of dollars a piece. Yet she has just launched her Simply Vera line of clothing in Coles stores across the US. The line's cardigans and jackets sell for US$60 to US$80, and US$120, respectively. Although this is still a lot of money, it shows that you can still own a piece of Vera for a relatively affordable price. We can only hope that Vera does the same thing in Australia. Check out Rina's story, below, for advice on making savings on your wardrobe.

Mum to mum

Nine months after the birth of my first child, I was due to go back to work. I hadn't bought any work clothes in the past two years. I figured I really needed a good pair of trousers, a skirt and three shirts to carry me through. A few weeks before I was to go back to work, I started looking around for clothes. I ended up in Target, and bought a shirt, trousers and skirt — all for under $100. I then bought another two shirts from Noni B on sale. I couldn't believe I'd spent under $130 on my work wardrobe.

Before my daughter was born, I would shop in boutique stores around the city and not really think about the cost. I wouldn't think twice about spending $150 on pair on trousers, for instance. Things are so different these days. After my son was born, money

Mum to mum (cont'd)

was tight because I hadn't worked for nine months — so I was really happy with my bargain workwear. The money that I saved on clothes I was able to spend on a great pair of shoes.

Rina, mother of two

Below is another story from another woman who has managed to save bundles of cash on her clothes. She is lucky enough to be a size 8 too!

Mum to mum

I work from home, and unless I have to go out for a meeting, I wear jeans for the most part. But jeans are so expensive; I can't justify paying up to $100 for a pair. I discovered that the St Vincent de Paul charity stores have a great range of jeans, and, being a size 8, I have found that the organisation has plenty to offer.

I have bought a few pairs of jeans from there. I paid only $5 for a pair of Levi's jeans once. The jeans were in excellent condition. It works for me. I told all the mums at school, and they just looked at me in disbelief.

I figure that the money I save by buying jeans from St Vinnies I can use to pay my local seamstress to adjust my clothes. I'd rather pay for someone to alter my clothes so that they fit just right, particularly because I'm slim. Also, the dressmaker has some great one-off dresses on display. I'm happy to go to her and pay for one of those dresses, knowing she will adjust it to fit my shape. The other night my husband and I went out for a special event, and I felt great, because I wore an outfit that fitted perfectly. For me it's worth it. I can save on some items, like jeans, and then lash out on something special just for me.

Laura, mother of two

Say no to ironing—a real time drainer

Whenever I buy an item of clothing, I make sure it won't need ironing. Fabrics have come a long way; you can now find great clothes that need very little, if any, ironing. Not having to iron is one thing I am adamant about. My aversion to ironing stems from being the eldest of six kids and being given the task of ironing when I was growing up at home.

Nowadays I buy very few clothes that require ironing, short of a few shirts and the kids' clothes. As soon as the clothes are washed, I shake them out and hang them on the line so that they dry in shape. Who has time for ironing? I know there are a million things I would rather do!

Cut back on your dry-cleaning

I also try to avoid buying clothes that require dry-cleaning. It's not just the cost that hurts; finding the time to take clothes to the drycleaners and then remembering to pick them up is hard as well. I have a friend who has done this so often that she's vowed never to take things to the drycleaners again.

Top tip: bargain mindsets

Remember: a bargain is only a bargain if you needed the item in the first place.

I understand that at times you will have stubborn stains on your favourite clothes, but before you head to the drycleaners, try some dry-cleaning fluid on the stains. You may be able to remove them yourself. I've done this a number of times, and it does the trick. You'll find dry-cleaning fluid in most hardware stores and major retailers.

Ponder point

I'm not a big clothing or accessory shopper, and I don't treat myself that often. So I try to indulge in some simple things, such as soaking in a hot bath. What I've started doing is turning some music on and sitting in the bath with a glass of wine. For me this is pure luxury. I just shut my eyes, and for the next ten to fifteen minutes, I savour every moment. When I get out, I feel lighter and incredibly relaxed. I try to have one at the end of the week — late at night when the kids are settled, so that I don't have to worry about hearing, 'Mum, can I have...?'. It's simple, but it works for me.

Below are some of my favourite tips for maximising fashion spend. Remember to:

- *buy on sale only.* I know I advocate this a lot, but it really is a mantra to live by. I'm particularly fond of the January sales. This is when you can grab a bargain, because stores across the nation slash prices to make way for the new season's stock. This is also a great time to purchase gifts to give as birthday presents later in the year. While you are at the January sales, start a gift box. When you see items such as books, music and movie DVDs, wines and general items on sale, put them aside, because they make great gifts for adults, young teenagers and kids.
- *set an annual clothing budget for yourself.* It can be hard to keep track of the money you spend on clothes, be they for yourself or your children. It therefore pays to keep track of what you spend each year; you will be surprised to find out how much money you spend on clothes.
- *leave it out if in doubt.* So often we buy on impulse and then regret it later. Consider whether you need what you want to buy before you buy it. The last you need in your wardrobe is items you don't wear taking up valuable space.
- *choose quality over quantity at all costs.* Having a pair of good shoes is preferable to owning several cheap pairs that won't last — costing you in the long run. The same applies with clothes: buy good-quality clothes rather than cheap and flimsy ones that will lose shape after one wash. As my mother

always said to me, 'Cheap will cost you in the long run'. This is why I wait until quality clothes are on sale before I buy them.

- *buy clothing in dark colours.* Dark clothes suit most people, and, on top of this, they're slimming!

Factory outlet stores

Don't forget the factory outlet stores. If you happen to live near one of them and getting there is easy, head out when you can. For those who don't live near one, put a day (or even half a day) aside to stock up. You can find genuine savings on designer labels — just as Sussane does (read her story below).

Mum to mum

I've been to the factory outlet stores a number of times, and I have saved quite a lot of money doing this. One time I went out with my daughter and bought shoes for her and me. Because I spent over $150, I was given a very smart, black handbag as a gift.

I've also bought a shirt for my husband from Nautica. It was blue linen and reduced from $399 to $99. He loves the shirt and wears it all the time.

Another time I went out to buy wedding and Christmas gifts. I bought a beautiful glass bowl that was valued at $200 but reduced in price to $99. It was a well-known brand of Japanese glass. The Christmas gifts I bought included items from Royal Doulton, Wedgwood and Villeroy & Boch.

The last time I went out, I bought myself a $400 skirt from Jigsaw that I paid $99 for. I also bought a little top to go with it for $12, which was a reduction from $40.

Sussane, mother of one

Great web buys

One of the best things about shopping online is that you can do it any time. Best of all, you can do it without the kids constantly asking, 'Are we done yet?' Sure, there is a risk that some of the clothes won't fit as well as you thought they might, but if you use some of the more established online retailers, you will probably be able to return them. Just make sure that you keep your receipts, that the items to be returned are in their original condition and that you have all the tags. If you're browsing a website and unsure about whether to purchase a product, check the site's return policy and guarantee section. Below are a few websites that will save you dollars.

- <*www.designeronline.com.au*>. Designer Online is an Australian company that provides an extensive range of authentic designer products at discounted prices. It offers men's and women's fragrances from perfume houses around the world, as well as handbags and accessories from internationally famous brands. By using a number of authorised distributors in Europe, the US and Canada, it is able to keep its costs down — and pass the savings on to you
- <*www.glamourgirl.com.au*>. Glamour Girl is a direct retailer of fashion jewellery, accessories and fun summer dresses

sourced from a huge range of international and Australian manufacturers. The site offers fast Express Post shipping on all orders, and free shipping in Australia on purchases over $100. This site boasts that you can save at least 25 per cent on retail prices.

- *<www.salesguide.com.au>*. This is another interesting site. It has been set up to inform shoppers of the best sales across Australia. It features sales on not only handbags, clothes and accessories but also children's toys. Once you register with the site, you'll receive emails detailing when and where to find the best sales.

eBay

The eBay revolution is here to stay. Because there are 21 million hits on eBay a month, you'd be hard-pressed to find a person who hasn't yet bought or sold anything on eBay!

The idea of shopping on eBay is great. Most people find they can grab a bargain on it. I've heard a number of cases of women buying designer clothes off eBay and then reselling them on it at a profit. If you're looking for some extra ways to earn money, this can work—and all you need is a computer and an internet connection.

Freshen up your wardrobe by adding one new item of clothing at the start of each season.

Hold a clothes party

Using the same concept behind make-up and Tupperware parties, why not hold a clothes party? The idea is to buy good-quality clothes from op shops, second-hand stores, vintage stores and eBay, and then sell them to your friends. Vicki did this and made a $130 profit. If she did this three times a year, she'd make almost $400 — a good way to find funds to treat herself. Read Vicki's story below.

Mum to mum

A friend of mine held a vintage clothes party, and I thought it was a good idea, so I decided to do the same. I bought some things at online auctions, and rummaged through second-hand stores and bins at St Vinnies. I had a budget of $150. I then asked friends and colleagues over for a clothes party. Some of the items I bought cost me no more than $10, and a few were designer labels that I thought I would auction off to see if I could get a good price for them.

At the end of the party, I tallied my takings for the day and found I'd made a profit of $130. I was quite happy with this, and decided I would hold more clothes parties — using the profits to reward myself. It took a little effort to get them up and running, but I did treat myself to a body massage with some of the profits. The rest of the money I used to buy more clothes for the next party.

It was a lot of fun. Plus, the girls who came along appreciated the fact that the items were so cheap. It's a good way to recycle clothes and make a little money on the side.

Vicki, mother of one

Do it yourself

Have you ever considered making your own clothes? Before you start saying that you don't have time, think hard and long about its benefits.

A friend of mine is a working mother with two girls. One way she likes to take time out—and this really gives her great pleasure—is by making her own clothes. I can attest to the fact that her clothes look fantastic. Sewing allows her to unleash her creativity—and it's a far cry from the hectic corporate world that occupies her weekdays. Of course, not all of us have the talent to make clothes, but if you do, start sewing. My friend's home-made clothes look like they've come straight off the rack of a designer. You'd never know the difference.

One advantage of making your own clothes it that it will save you money

One advantage of making your own clothes is that it will save you money. The other advantage is that it will allow you to do something for yourself—something that you can take pride in because it is the result of your creativity.

Accessories

I'm a big fan of using accessories to transform an outfit. Doing this is a lot cheaper than buying new clothes. If you choose wisely, your accessories will stand the test of time—which is better than buying into the fashion trends each season.

Today you can rummage through markets, second-hand stores and vintage stores to find some of the most unusual and inexpensive pieces. Or, if you want to unleash your creativity, why not make your jewellery? Kelly, for example, did just this. She was at a loss after changing careers and wanted to do something that would allow her to work from home and be with her daughter. Her love of jewellery turned into a thriving business — as shown below.

Mum to mum

What got me started [in jewellery making] was an ad I saw for a beading course in my local area. I had always loved jewellery and thought it would be something I would enjoy learning about. I'd finished working part time as a travel agent, and I decided to do this course at night, which fitted in with my having a child.

My husband would look after our daughter while I attended the course. After one year, I started making jewellery for friends and family. The handmade designs really caught on; I started selling the jewellery at a number of markets. Now my jewellery business has taken off. I also make custom-made pieces for my clients.

Kelly, mother of two

As you can see from this chapter, there are many ways you can save on your wardrobe and accessory needs. Indeed, some of the tips in this chapter will not only help you cut costs but also give you a chance to feel great.

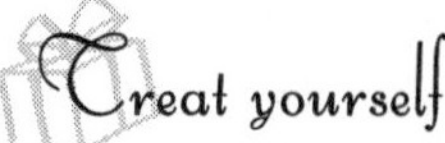

Treat yourself

Try some of the following pick-me-ups. They will save you money and help you feel good too.

- *Take a sewing course so that you can make your own clothes.* Lose yourself in creativity and save some money at the same time by creating your own outfits. Learn to sew at one of the many TAFE colleges or your local community centre.
- *Start a beading course.* Get creative and make your own individual pieces. If beading isn't your thing, take a course in another type of jewellery making. If you become really good, you may like to try selling your wares at a market, as Kelly did (her story is on page 135).
- *Scout for a bargain item.* We all take pleasure in finding an item we've always wanted, particularly when it's been reduced.
- *Rejuvinate yourself by decluttering your wardobe and finding clothes for the next season.* If you're unsure about what to keep and what to throw out, ask some friends over and get their advice.
- *Buy clothes in black and white.* A must-have in any wardrobe is a well-cut pair of black trousers and a white shirt. These two items can be adapted to any situation. Actress Faye Dunaway immortalised chic workwear in the movie *Network*, in which she wore a classic white shirt and black skirt throughout.

- *Invest in some new pyjamas*. That's right, get rid of the oversized T-shirts and slip into some of the fun, affordable sleepwear designs available in stores.

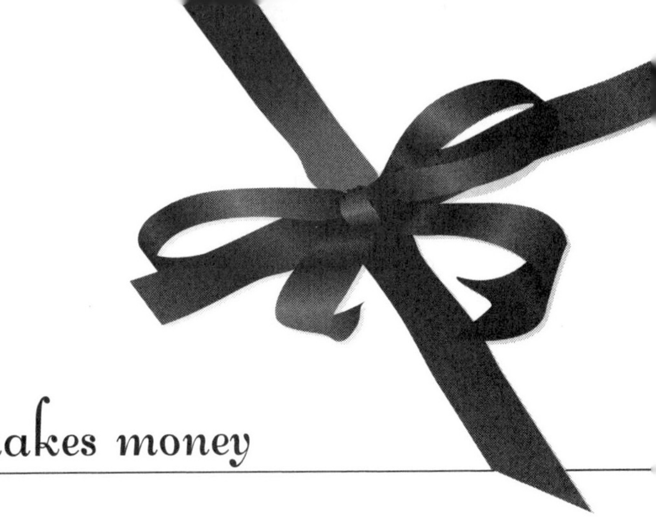

Chapter 8

Money makes money

In chapter 6 I show you ways to help you teach your children about money. This chapter will help you understand why money makes money (that is, investment), along with showing you simple ways to build your assets.

Everyone's perspective on money varies, and depending on where your finances are at this moment in your life, that perspective can be positive or negative. It can be influenced by the way you remember money being handled in your family when you were growing up. For example, if your family had plenty of money and you never witnessed your parents being worried about paying bills, it would have had an impact on you. The same goes if you watched your family struggling to make ends meet, or if you grew up in a household that never discussed money (so you were not aware of what was happening around you). It's no wonder that many children grow up without good money-management skills.

It's important to have a positive view of money but not an obsessive one. Don't simply fall into the trap of making money; instead, learn how to make your money work for you. It is equally important to take the time to enjoy what you've worked to achieve.

It really doesn't matter how much money you have; it's what you do with your cash that counts

True 'wealth' means possessing a healthy balance—surrounding yourself with family, friends and a job you enjoy. Money gives you the opportunity and freedom to spend on yourself and your loved ones. It allows you to spend on something as simple as a gorgeous shirt that caught your eye, a weekend away for the family, or a meal at a fancy restaurant with your partner so that you can enjoy some time alone.

It really doesn't matter how much money you have; it's what you do with your cash that counts. I know people who earn plenty of money but are always broke! On the other hand, I also know people who don't earn much but who are smart enough to make their money work for them.

The principles of investing

Sound investing begins with knowing what you want out of life. Some people are happy to own their home and have enough money put aside for a rainy day. Others want to build wealth and invest.

Either way, you must understand what you really want for yourself. Investing is not for everyone; it takes a certain amount of risk and commitment. However, you can reduce that risk by learning about about investing (more on that later in the chapter).

So if your plan is to invest and grow your money, you must clear all your debts first — by this I mean personal debts, such as credit card debts and high-interest loans. There is no point putting money aside and trying to build wealth when your bills are increasing and you're barely making the minimum payments.

Also, you should start investing with a clear conscious about your finances. Once you know that your bills are under control and that you're managing your mortgage payments, you should feel better about putting money aside to invest. Basically, you must be able to rest easy at night rather than worrying about your investments as you lie awake in bed. Investing can be summed up in the following three steps:

1 Plan

2 Educate yourself

3 Know your investment profile.

Plan

I touched on planning earlier, when I said that you'll need to know what you want for yourself. Once you understand what you want from your investments, you can proceed to build an investment plan. Whichever investment type you choose — be it shares, property or managed funds — be prepared to invest for the long term (ideally any time from five years and up).

Think of investing as starting a business: you wouldn't expect to start a business and then finish up within a year or so, would you? Treat investing the same way—put the time in and plan well, and you will be rewarded.

A financial planner is also a good investment, but I would advise you to educate yourself as much as possible before you visit one so that you'll know the right questions to ask. Visit the Financial Planning Association of Australia (FPA) at <www.fpa.asn.au> to find a financial planner in your area. Also, the FPA's website has a fantastic booklet called 'Don't kiss your money goodbye'. In it you'll find practical information about financial advisers, along with all the questions you'll need to ask. You may also like to ask your friends or colleagues if they can recommend an adviser for you to use.

Educate yourself

Educating yourself about investing is one of the most important step to take before you invest. Before I began my journey into understanding the basics of investing, I knew nothing. This was about fifteen years ago, when there was little information out there, particularly for women. Many of my female friends were in the same position. Little did I know that about five years later, I would start an investment club with my female colleagues and help write a best-selling book, *The Money Club*, about my experience, which spurred on hundreds of women to start their own clubs!

When it comes to investing, the backing of a support group is a great way to learn. Whether it is in the form of a structured gathering, such as an investment club, or simply a get-together of like-minded friends with whom you are comfortable talking about money, a support group will help.

Courses and seminars are excellent forums to learn. I attended a few of these seminars when I was starting out. To help get you started, the Australian Securities Exchange (ASX) offers lots of courses for beginners. Go to <www.asx.com.au> for more information. The site includes general introductory courses on investing, as well as specific information on different types of investments. Another good website to visit is the Australian Shareholders' Association's (ASA), at <www.asa.asn.au>. The ASA offers regular seminars, discussion groups and educational DVDs.

The other thing that helped me was reading the finance section in the newspaper. I know the finance section is not the most riveting read, but if you really want to learn about and understand how the world of investing works, it's a good strategy. I also kept my eye out for the 'money supplements' in the larger newspapers that are aimed at your average 'mum and dad' investors. Books are another great way to gain knowledge. There are dozens of books on investing in the major bookstores. For young women, my book *The Savvy Girl's Money Book* is a great place to start, and *Shopping for Shares*, by Tracey Edwards, is another good buy for women looking to invest. It pays to spend some time going through the books available, so that you will find one you can relate to. You may want to borrow books from the library to see what you like, prior to purchasing.

Know your investment profile

Before you're ready to invest, it's really important to know what sort of investor you are and what your investing profile is.

Are you risk-averse or a risk-taker? Do you want to build wealth but require a low-risk option? Once you've assessed your profile, you need to understand the types of investment vehicles on offer to help you decide where to put your money. For example, are you an investor—what I call a 'Clayton's investor'—who doesn't really want to spend the time learning about investing? If so, the easiest option could be to simply top up your superannuation. If you do this, at least you will be on your way to ensuring you have enough money for retirement. The closer you are to retirement age, the more appealing this will be, thanks to the recent changes to superannuation laws. The changes to superannuation have reduced many of the taxes that were once in place. There is more on superannuation on page 151.

Successful investors usually invest in something that takes their interest

To give you a better understanding of the areas you can invest in to build wealth, read about the most common investment options, shown below.

- shares
- managed funds
- property
- cash-management accounts
- superannuation.

There's no harm in trying a few of these at once; most experts agree that diversifying your investments is a smart move. Successful investors usually invest in something that takes their interest. It's important to know which investment type suits your profile.

Shares

When you purchase shares in a company, you are buying a small portion of the ownership of that company. In other words, you become a shareholder.

Shares can be bought through a brokerage company. Try online trading brokers such as <www.comsec.com.au> and <www.etrade.com.au>, or go through a private brokerage company. Shares come with a certain amount of risk, so you need to understand, at the very least, the basics of how the sharemarket works before you invest. One of the most valuable lessons I've learned since investing is to invest for the long haul.

Before I began investing in shares, I spent a lot of time reading books and attending seminars, as well as speaking to other investors. Lynelle relates her experience of educating herself about shares below.

Mum to mum

When I was eighteen, my uncle, who was a stockbroker, taught me how to invest in the sharemarket. It was one of the best lessons I ever learned about investing. I bought mainly blue-chip shares, such as shares in IAG and Commonwealth Bank. I continued investing throughout my career, and I retired at the age of 50. I'm 52 now, and I've been living off the dividends from my investments.

Lynelle, mother of two

Managed funds

Managed funds offer another way for you to create wealth. One of the major benefits of investing in managed funds is that it takes all the guesswork out of deciding where to invest. Managed funds are operated by professional fund managers. Once you buy into a managed fund, the fund pools your money with that of other investors in the fund. You can start investing with a relatively small amount. With most managed funds, you can expect to pay an entry fee of up to 4 per cent and ongoing fees ranging from 1.5 to 2.5 per cent per annum. Some funds offer no fees if you join online.

There are dozens and dozens of funds to choose from, and they cover a number of different industries. You can buy into Australian funds or international funds. You'll find a comprehensive list of managed funds every Wednesday in the *Australian Financial Review.* The star rating beside each of the funds listed will give you an indication of how the fund is performing. You can track how it is going via its percentage returns across a certain period (one year, three years or five years). Another website to visit that lists top-performing growth funds is Morningstar Australia's, found at <www.morningstar.com.au>. Check out Lana's experience of managed funds:

Mum to mum

My partner and I are currently paying off our home. After working through our budget, we found that we had a surplus of $50 a week. We decided to speak to a financial adviser, and she *recommended that we use the money to invest in a managed fund. Because we are only young (both of us are 32), she suggested that we start the fund with $1000, and then continue with regular monthly contributions of $100 or $200. We took the advice. Now we have been contributing for over a year. We chose a fund that had reasonable returns, and we expect to make a return of approximately 10.5 per cent per annum over five years.*

My goal would be to keep up the contributions as long as possible. This is important to us because we plan to have another child in two years, and we may not have the extra money around when we have another mouth to feed. I'm really glad we're doing something with the extra $50.

Lana, mother of one

Cash-management accounts

Most cash-management accounts are suitable for either short- or long-term investing. These types of investments can work well if you are planning for a holiday or saving for a deposit on a home. A number of institutions offer online accounts, which are generally linked to transaction accounts. Online accounts offer a number of advantages, including the provision of bonus interest if you only make a deposit and don't withdraw any money for the month. Also, you don't need a lot of money to start these investments, although some accounts do require a minimum initial investment amount. Most of the major banks offer cash-management accounts, and you can easily set one up online by visiting the website of the financial institution you prefer (go to <www.abetterdeal.com.au> or <www.ingdirect.com.au> to see some good options). Expect to receive about 7 per cent interest on your investment. Cash-management accounts are a good option for low-risk investors.

Property

Arguably the biggest investment you will make is buying the family home. Australians love to own property—almost 70 per cent of us own some form of property. Compare this with European nations, where homeownership is much lower because people are more content to rent for the rest of their lives. Take Germany, for example, where homeownership is just under 45 per cent. It's understandable that Australians want to own a home in a country surrounded by glorious coastline. Who wouldn't want a piece of that pie?

Property investing will work really well for you if you do your homework

One of the advantages of investment properties is that they provide you with returns in two ways—rent and capital growth. There are many books and seminars on investing in property. *The Power of Property,* by Karina Barrymore and Bruce Brammall, is a good book to start with.

Property investing will work really well for you if you do your homework. The golden rule for investing in property is 'location, location, location', particularly if you are investing in residential property.

Before you purchase an investment property, study the property market in your area. View lots and lots of properties. (I know someone who viewed almost a hundred properties before she bought her first one.) Make sure the area of your choice is on an upward trend in terms of property value. If possible, check out the rental listings in the area. If you notice dozens of apartments for rent, it could be a warning that the area is not a good choice for property investment.

Don't be afraid to dedicate time to research before you purchase. Nobody ever lost money taking too much time, but rushing into a decision could cost you dearly. This goes for any investment. Rachelle is one property investor who knows the value of research. Read her story below.

Mum to mum

My husband and I were keen to build wealth. Both of us have good jobs. I told him that I wanted to invest in property. He was very supportive, and we agreed that we would leverage the equity in our home to purchase an investment unit. We bought our first investment unit almost eight years ago; today we have five small apartments, which are all rented out.

I wasn't interested in investing in the sharemarket because I like to see what I'm buying — it's just the way I am. Initially I set a target to purchase four units within a seven-year time frame. It took a lot of commitment, but I absolutely loved trawling around the units for sale every Saturday morning.

My husband would joke that I bought units the way women buy clothes. He was right in a sense, because it was shopping, just on a larger scale.

The lesson I learned was to buy property in areas that are close to transport and community services. I chose to buy my units in

Mum to mum (cont'd)

suburbs close to the city. I always looked for units that were a little run-down. Then I would do some cosmetic touch-ups. I'm really happy with that decision, and it was great to have the support of my husband. He really had faith in me that I could do it on my own — he certainly wasn't interested in spending Saturday mornings looking at property.

Owning six properties, including my home, is nothing to be sneezed at. In a few years, I hope to sell a couple of them to pay off the bank, and then just live off the rental income.

Rachelle, mother of two

Another way to share a slice of the property market is to invest in a managed property fund. It works like any investment fund in that you pool your money together with other investors. The only difference is that managed property funds invest in property.

Another way to share a slice of the property market is to invest in a managed property fund

This type of investment is worth considering if you are a hands-on investor who wants to invest in the property market without having to wait years for a rise in a particular property's value. The benefit of this is that it exposes you to the property market without you needing to take out a large mortgage, because you can invest with as little as $2000 — just like buying shares. You'll earn returns from your fund when property prices rise.

Top tip: tax

Because the returns on any investments are taxable, you'll need to declare any profit you make to the Australian Taxation Office (ATO). The profit is known as capital gain, and you may have to pay capital gains tax (CGT) on it. However, CGT can be offset against any losses you make on your investment in the same year. Please check with your accountant to receive an accurate assessment of what CGT you may have to pay.

Property funds comprise industrial, commercial and residential property. Expect to pay fees similar to those of other managed funds. The other benefit of this option is that you won't have to worry about paying the legal fees, stamp duty, maintenance costs and council rates that come with owning property.

Ponder point

I believe having the right balance between a man's and a woman's role is the key to happiness in any relationship. I look around at my friends who are happily married or partnered, and they give equally to the relationship. This goes for men as well. It seems to me that couples who are prepared to share the load and play an active role in parenting, work and the home are the happy ones.

Superannuation

As I mentioned earlier, investing is not for everyone. Thanks to the growth in the sharemarket over the last few years, the majority of superannuation funds have performed well. Use this opportunity to add and build your superannuation. If you want to make sure that you have enough money to live comfortably when you retire, make regular contributions to your superannuation fund because it is a relatively easy way to build a nest egg. We can thank former Australian prime minister Paul Keating for making superannuation compulsory.

Sadly, women, in particular, fall short when it comes to accumulating superannuation

As the population ages, many people start finding that their super will be their only means of retirement income. Sadly, women, in particular, fall short when it comes to accumulating superannuation. According to the Association of Superannuation Funds of Australia (ASFA), the average superannuation account payout balance is $130 000 for men and $45 000 for women. (Read more about this at <www.superannuation.asn.au>.)

Of course, there are a number of reasons for this, but, for women, it's largely due to the fact that we take time out to have children and when we do go back to work, it's mainly part time. Therefore, we tend not to receive the benefits associated with putting away as much super as possible.

The compulsory super contributions your employer pays on your behalf must make up 9 per cent of your income. By adding, say, an extra 1 or 2 per cent on top of your employer's regular contributions, you could add many thousands of dollars to your super income on retirement. Of course, that depends on how many regular contributions you make and how long you invest in the fund, thanks to compound interest. (Compound interest allows you to earn interest on your interest over the term of your investment. This means that the longer you save, the larger the return you'll make.)

The government is particularly generous with its superannuation co-contributions at the moment. For every dollar that people earning under $58 000 contribute to their super, they will receive $150 from the government. For more information on government co-contributions, visit <www.ato.gov.au>.

Below is an example of how two different women can earn significantly different incomes from their super funds. One has made no voluntary contributions and the other one has. We'll assume that both women have no prior superannuation in their kitty and that they each earn an average salary of $40 000. The figures show that if you choose to contribute 2 per cent of your income, above the compulsory 9 per cent contribution provided by your employer, you can accumulate almost an extra 25 per cent in your superannuation kitty on retirement.

Name	Kate	Sarah
Age	35	35
Retirement age	65	65
Salary	$40 000	$40 000
Return on super fund	7 per cent	7 per cent
Employer contributions	$3600	$3600
Voluntary contributions	$800	$0
Super balance at age 65	$185 000	$147 000

Imagine what you could do if you had an extra $38 000 at retirement! It could be enough to pay for home renovations, new appliances, a holiday or even a new car.

Top tip: lost super

Would you believe that one in three Australians has lost superannuation money? I'm not one of them, but you might be.

If you're like the many Australians who in the early stages of their career moved in and out of jobs and forgot to transfer their super contributions, ask yourself what happened to them.

Well the money is sitting in a pot of gold at Australia's Unclaimed Super Fund (AUSfund). There is over $1.5 million worth of lost super waiting to be claimed. To find out if you have super owing, log on to the AUSfund website at <www.unclaimedsuper.com.au>.

If you're not yet eligible for a super payout, then you can roll-over the money into your own superannuation fund. Any lost super that is under $200 can be claimed at any age and under any circumstances, and it's tax-free.

Invest in friends and money

Becoming a member of an investment club was one of the wisest investing decisions I ever made. I not only learned so much about investing in shares but also discovered the importance of having a support team to discuss investment.

One night at my book club, the book discussion took a back seat to discussing the prospect of running an investment club. We'd heard about investment clubs overseas, but there was very little information on them in Australia. From that one meeting, several book club members and I decided to start an investment club. We decided to use the same principles as our book club — plenty of good food, wine and conversation.

In 1998 the Sheba Investment Network was born, or, as we fondly refer to ourselves, SIN or SINNERS. There was so much interest in our group that we subsequently wrote *The Money Club* in 2001. The 'how to' guide to starting an investment club became a bestseller — so clearly there's a need out there for more information on investment clubs.

Having a group of friends who share the same values and concerns about their financial future is helpful

Starting up an investment portfolio on your own can be daunting, so having a group of friends who share the same values and concerns about the financial future is helpful. In my club, we know each well enough to talk about money issues; whenever anyone has an idea or a point she wishes to discuss, we value the person's feedback.

Investment clubs provide a great platform to learn about investing in the sharemarket, particularly if you do not have a lot of cash to invest initially. When we started our club ten years ago, we began with ten members. We decided to kick-start our contributions with $200 each, and then we contributed $50 a month after that. Six years later we chose to increase that to $75 a month. Today we each put in $100 a month. To date, we've had many happy returns. We have averaged a return of over 30 per cent.

Make your money work for you, so that you won't have to work as hard for it.

This is a very easy and affordable way to start investing — as you can see, you only need a few hundred dollars to get started. At the time we all decided that what we invested would go towards securing our financial future. Plus, the money we contributed each week was the equivalent of what we would normally spend on a night out.

Although most people form investment clubs to buy into the sharemarket, many others use the same structure to buy into property or managed funds. It doesn't matter which investing vehicle you choose for your club, the main aim is to make sure you all have the same investment philosophy and goals.

I know a group of five people who came together to invest in real estate in Queensland. The club started four years ago, after its members read *The Money Club*. The club now owns two properties and makes returns of approximately 25 per cent. The rental income the properties generate covers all maintentance costs. They are now very happy with their decision to start the club. It was the only way for them to ever afford property in Queensland.

Using investment clubs to treat yourself

The less obvious benefit of joining an investment club is that it allows you to widen your circle of friends and meet new people. Indeed, I even enjoyed a fabulous weekend away with my fellow club members. After three good years of returns from our shares, we decided to reward ourselves.

Every Christmas we enjoyed dining at any one of the city's finest restaurants, but after eight years of investing it was time for something more.

In June 2006, instead of meeting at a member's home each month, we would go out to dinner for our meetings; we did this for a year. Later we decided that it was time for a weekend away in the Hunter Valley — not just an ordinary weekend away but what we now call an 'extreme indulgence' weekend. We'd already had two weekends away as a group, but this time it was different. We enjoyed five-star accommodation, a limousine that took us around to the various vineyards in the valley and dinner at a top restaurant. To finish it off, we were pampered by spa and beauty treatments.

We started out as women who knew nothing about buying and selling shares; now we have our own investment portfolios

In the time our club's been together, we've had our fair share of ups and downs — just like the sharemarket. The biggest benefit for all of us was what we learned along the way. We started out as women who knew nothing about buying and selling shares; now we have our own investment portfolios. Some members started investing in superannuation funds, and others bought investment property.

When I think about my club, I never think about the money we've made; I usually recall the fun we've had. After all, the whole idea behind us starting the club was for us to make money so that we could take trips, have time out and enjoy a little fine dining.

For more information on investment clubs, or to start your own club with a Money Club kit, visit <www.themoneyclub.com.au>.

Treat yourself

Have a go at rewarding yourself in one of the following ways:

- *Go on a girls' night out.* How long has it been since you last had a girls' night out? It's great to get together with some close friends, let your hair down and have some fun.
- *Start a book club.* Book clubs are a great way to get together with friends and discuss topics other than children!
- *Launch a 'something different' club.* By this I mean you should try something different each month with a group of friends. I'm part of group called the 'something different group'. Each month we take turns at organising a night that allows us to do something we wouldn't normally do. Some of the things we've tried include:
    - a night at the observatory
    - salsa dancing

  - learning to cook seafood at a class at the local fish market
  - listening to a talk at the art gallery.

- *Set a date with your mum, and have a morning of coffee and cake.*

- *Take the income you've earned from your investment club and go on a luxury weekend with your friends.* Relax, unwind and indulge yourself at one of the island resorts. Leave your cares and worries behind. Spend the time lounging around the pool and sipping cocktails — the only work you'll do will be building up your tan.

Chapter 9

Healthy savings

As parents, we face many challenges throughout our lives to ensure our children grow into healthy, confident adults. There isn't one parent who has not spent a night at the emergency ward of a children's hospital. When there are broken limbs, flu-like symptoms or asthma attacks, we're off to the hospital in a flash — sometimes waiting for hours before our children are seen. This is part and parcel of being a parent; our job is take care of our kids — when they fall, we're there to pick them up. But you need to look after yourself too, for your kids' sake as well as your own.

In this chapter you'll see ways to make sure you receive the pick-me-up to help you keep going. You'll see how other mums manage to fit exercise into their day to rejuvinate themselves. Hopefully, it will inspire you to incorporate at least one of their suggestions into your routine.

The other areas in this chapter look at ways you can cut back on health expenses — after all, they do make up a considerable portion of household bills. I also show you some tactics for maximising the returns on your health insurance and pharmacy items, and, in turn, using those savings to help you look and feel good.

Who's looking after you?

So much of our time as mothers is consumed by the demands of kids, work and home. Finding time to keep our bodies and minds at an optimum does require some effort.

It doesn't matter what form of exercise you prefer; the important thing is to find the time to do it. For some, a heavy workout at the gym may be the answer; for others, a brisk walk is enough to reinvigorate a tired body and mind.

All forms of exercise help to nurture our spirits in a positive way, and this will affect all areas of your life — your kids will notice it too.

Ponder point

Understand that making yourself a priority is not about being selfish. Think of yourself as a well: if you continue to take water from the well without replenishing it, it will run dry. We owe it to our children, our partners and, most of all, ourselves. Remember not to beat yourself up for taking time out. Take pleasure in knowing that you are doing something for the good of your health and wellbeing. Invest in ten minutes of relaxation a day — something as simple as embracing the stillness of meditation does wonders.

Vitamins and health products

We all know how costly it is to keep healthy and have all our vitamins. Thankfully, a number of online pharmacies offer pharmaceutical and health products at affordable prices. Below are a few Australian companies. The main benefit of these websites is that they will ship to anywhere in Australia. Plus, all their products are certified for sale in Australia, which means you won't have to worry about your product being confiscated by customs as you would if you purchased from overseas pharmaceutical sites.

- *<www.discountvitaminsexpress.com.au>*. DVE's online services offers a comprehensive list of products. It stocks over 4000 items from most brand names, including health supplements at discounted prices, as much as 20 per cent off retail prices.
- *<www.thexton.com.au>*. ThextonHealth is a supplier of health and nutritional products. It delivers across Australia, usually within two to three days. It offers regular discounts on its products and will notify you of specials once you become a member.

Top tip: free health services

It's time to check in with you. Running a busy household can take its toll on your health. Are you spending enough time looking

Top tip (cont'd): free health services

after yourself? Or are you focusing only on the health of the rest of the family? You must keep yourself healthy. So take advantage of some of the free health services offered to women, such as those provided by BreastScreen Australia.

BreastScreen Australia provides free mammograms to all women over 40, and specifically targets women aged 50 to 69. To make an appointment for a mammogram at your nearest BreastScreen Australia service, phone 13 20 50 or visit <www.breastscreen.info.au> for further information.

Ways to invigorate yourself

When was the last time you took time out without feeling a twinge of guilt? That long, huh? Studies reveal that men have an hour's leisure time a day. What about you? Now is the time to improve your mental and physical health. The suggestions in this section provide easy and affordable ways to exercise your body and mind. The only guilt you should feel is about why you didn't try them sooner.

Top tip: time for you

Make sure you slot in time for yourself, even if it's something as simple as ten minutes of meditation. Write it down in your diary, because writing it down is a powerful way to form a habit. I find this really does work.

Join a gym

Thank goodness there are so many gyms offering child care on site. It means that you can no longer let your little ones stop you from keeping fit. So consider joining your local gym. After all, you need abundant energy to get through being a parent. Read Lesley's experience of joining a gym, below.

Mum to mum

I value my gym membership because it gives me some me time, and helps me to relax and recharge.

I can justify spending $33 per fortnight on it by breaking the membership figure down into how much each visit costs. So if I go three times a week, I know it works out costing me $5 a go, which is very cheap.

Lesley, mother of two

Do it yourself

If the gym is not your thing and you can't take the time to travel to one, then plan a workout for yourself. Doing this may be the way for you to go because it enables you to get fit at any time of the day. For example, since the birth of my second son, Marc, I've been getting up early in the morning to do my exercise, which is generally a brisk walk followed by stretching. Read Lynette's story, overleaf, for more on the importance of keeping fit.

Mum to mum

Six years ago I saw a photo of myself with my young daughter, who was six months old at the time. We were both on the couch, and I was wearing my usual wardrobe at the time, which was a burgundy tracksuit. What struck me was how tired I looked in the photo — my face had no vibrancy. I was 39 at the time and had three children. The wear and tear of raising them showed on my face. I decided it was time to get 'me' back. I made a plan, really a pact with myself, that no matter what, I would change the way I felt. If it meant I needed to get up and exercise at 5.30 am I would; on the other hand, if it meant I would have to do it at 8.00 pm I would. I designed a routine that I could do on my own at any time of the day. What it also gave me was time for myself — something I'd completely forgotten about.

Lynette, mother of three

You may even want to start a do-it-yourself exercise routine with a few like-minded friends, just as Rhonda did. (See her story below.) The important thing is to do something.

Mum to mum

I attended my first mothers' group when my daughter was six weeks old ... I feel very fortunate to have such a wonderful mothers' group. They are all kind, patient, understanding, helpful and, most of all, supportive.

After the first few months of our babies' lives, we all felt the same: tired, tired and more tired. By this stage, I thought it was time to get back to my training routine. My gym membership had lapsed months before, and, with a little one, I knew it was going to be difficult to get to and from the gym. So I decided to start training in my local park. I would do a workout — a combination of running and training — for an hour. When I told the girls in my mothers' group, a few of them were interested in training with me. So we agreed to meet two nights a week, or when possible.

The evenings proved to be the best time — when the hubbies came home, we had a chance to escape. We'd meet in the park between 6.30 pm and 7.00 pm. Regardless of the cold and the dark, we were committed to spending an hour running, boxing, and doing lots of cardio and endurance training.

At the end of each session, even though we were exhausted, we all felt so great. Exercise really helps to release all that stress and tension. When you finish, you can go back into the house to face everything — and it seems a lot easier to handle.

Everything about our exercise was positive: it's free, we get an hour to ourselves and we work hard. It's time for us, and you really can't do this when you have children with you. Sure, it's nice to go for a walk with the bub, but getting together with friends to exercise is a completely different feeling. And, best of all, you are getting fit and losing that weight, especially around the mid-section.

It's getting a little harder now due to most of us returning to work, but we do it when we can, whether there is two, four or more of us.

Rhonda, mother of one

Meditation

Having the ability to sit in silence and give in to your surroundings is a real gift. The serene faces of Buddhist monks attest to this. Meditation is something I have always longed to master — and Maria is one mum who has (read her story below).

Mum to mum

The first thing I do in the morning is start stretching and meditating for five minutes — I do this before going for my run. I then have a healthy breakfast of muesli, yoghurt and fruit, followed by a top-up of my vitamins. It doesn't take much, but I do feel it allows me to start my day with my mind and body working at the optimum.

Maria, mother of two

Meditation helps calm the mind and spirit. When you keep thinking about all the things you have to do, meditation may just be what you need. Give yourself at least ten minutes a day — perhaps first thing in the morning before you busy day begins. Kristen knows the value of meditation. Read her story below.

Mum to mum

I've been working on nurturing myself a little lately. One of the books I'm reading is Buddhism for Mothers. *It's really resonating with me. One of the things the book encourages is meditation, so I've been trying it. I have a meditation CD I listen to and have been trying to steal 20 minutes every day to meditate. I'm pretty terrible at keeping my focus (my mind wanders quite a bit), but I must say that I am enjoying it, and I find it gives me a little pep. I've put my meditation recording on my iPod, and I try to listen to it whenever and wherever I can. One great spot is the kids' trampoline — you kind of feel like you are floating.*

Kristen, mother of two

Yoga and Pilates

The popularity of yoga and Pilates continue to grow every year. If you have ever practised either of these, then you are aware of the benefits they offer. Yoga and Pilates provides a great stress release for the body; they also build your strength. It really doesn't matter if you cannot find the time to do a full workout. Half an hour, or even ten minutes, of poses, can be beneficial. I found the best way to get my yoga stretches down pat was to buy an instructional DVD. There are many available, and they cater for everyone from beginners and advanced practitioners to time-poor mums. Read about how Jenny fits yoga into her busy day in the box below.

Mum to mum

For my last birthday my sister bought me a yoga DVD. She knew how time-poor I was, so she bought me a DVD specifically designed for busy people. It's called 10 Minute Solution Yoga. *It has five easy workouts, from basic yoga to yoga stretches — all*

Mum to mum (cont'd)

designed to be done within ten minutes. I decided I'd do it early in the morning. When you think about it, ten minutes goes really quickly. I've started using it every second day. It's great — I wish there were more things designed to give you a lift in ten minutes.

Jenny, mother of one

Health insurance — cut out the extras

To really make the most of your private health insurance, you need to assess if you require the level of cover you have.

Take a look at all the ancillary cover, or 'extras'; do you really need them all? The best way to do this is to look back over the last couple of years and see if you used any of your insurance extras — for example, cover for optical, dental, chiropractic or pregnancy. Then add up what those extras cost you each year. So if you have been paying $800 for extras and you only spent $400 on them, consider whether the cover is worthwhile. On the other hand, you do not want to be caught out in the future by not having enough insurance to cover certain things, such as major dental work.

These days many health insurance policies offer tailored cover, so you can ensure you are paying only for what you need

These days many health insurance policies offer tailored cover, so you can ensure you are paying only for what you need. Remember that the needs of a family are different from those of singles and retirees.

If you are unsure about whether your policy is meeting the needs of your family, then compare the funds out there to see your other options. Go to <www.iselect.com.au>. It allows you to compare your existing health policy with others, hopefully helping you save on health insurance.

Also, don't forget to keep all your Medicare, doctor and hospital bills. Once you've spent over $1500, you will receive a rebate in your tax return.

Pregnant pause

Like many, you have probably been receiving regular letters about increases to your health fund. It's easy to let the reminders come through and simply pay them automatically (like many mums, you've probably had the same health cover for a number of years).

Last year, after receiving yet another notice of a fee increase to my health insurance, I decided to ring my health insurance provider to find out exactly what I was paying for and if there were any areas I could cut back on to reduce my premium. I discovered that I had been paying for extra cover for pregnancy and obstetrics. I had completely overlooked this — my youngest son was ten and I had no plans to have any more children. To my surprise and annoyance, I discovered this extra cover was costing me $100 a quarter. I immediately put a stop to the cover and saved $400 a year as a result. I realised that if I had stopped this cover ten years earlier, I would have saved myself the equivalent of $4000. Argh! I'd been paying for cover that I no longer required.

I also discovered I was not alone. A friend of mine had exactly the same issue. She saved $50 a month, or $600 a year, after realising she'd been paying for pregnancy cover she no longer needed.

Protecting your income

I believe income protection insurance, sometimes called disability protection cover, is one of the most important types of cover parents should have. You never know when you are going to fall ill or have an accident — leaving your family without your income while you recover. Income protection is particularly important for single mums who work and suddenly find themselves having to take time off due to illness. Ask yourself, 'Who will pay the bills if I cannot work for several months?'

If you're taking out income protection cover, make sure it will cover you for the job you actually perform. Most policies will provide you with ongoing income worth up to 75 per cent of the salary you usually receive. Best of all, income protection insurance is tax-deductible.

Visit <www.cannex.com.au> to see the range of income protection policies that are available. Anna's experience, shown in the box below, demonstrates why having income protection cover is a very good idea.

Mum to mum

When I was pregnant with my first child, I had severe nausea. This was caused by the unusually high hormone levels in my body.

Here I was expecting to be happy about being pregnant, when at five weeks I started to feel very unwell. I struggled with going into the office because I had to rush to the toilet every hour to throw up. At six weeks' pregnant, the nausea and headaches became so bad that I could not get out of bed. I really thought I was going mad. I rang the office and told my boss the news. I spent the next five weeks in bed — sometimes I would even have to rush to the hospital to be put on a drip due to the dehydration.

I was worried about whether I could go back to work. We had a baby on the way, and I needed to keep working for the income. I contacted my income protection company and found my policy would cover my time off. It's times like these that you are so grateful to have a policy in place — when you really, really need it.

Anna, mother of one

I hope you've used this chapter to find some great ways to save on your health needs. Remember, looking after yourself is just important as looking after your family.

Treat yourself

If you're feeling frazzled, try doing one of the following activities to receive a lift:

- *Drink water.* I know this tip is an obvious one, but when I'm under pressure I try to steer away from coffee and stick with

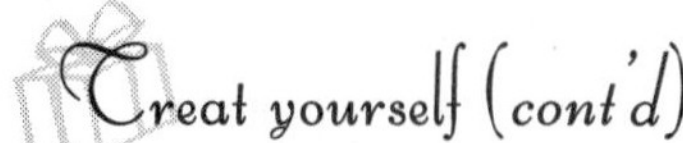

Treat yourself (cont'd)

water instead. Stress causes dehydration, so keep your fluids up. Mums are always concerned about whether their kids are getting enough water, so make sure you show the same concern for yourself.

- *Stock up on herbal teas, vitamins, protein drinks, nuts and energy foods.* Then if you feel like you need a lift, you'll have a supply of energy-building fuel on hand.
- *Throw out the oversized T-shirts and daggy, old trackpants, and replace them with some new exercise gear (including running shoes).* You don't need to go over the top; buy enough to make you feel good about yourself.
- *Buy some essential oils.* They not only heighten your aromatic senses but also offer other therapeutic benefits. These wonderful oils can either stimulate or sedate the central nervous system. You need a small oil burner — just add a few droplets of the essential oil to it. The oils burn for up to eight hours. Take a look at the ones below; they are designed to have a particular effect on you.
    - peppermint, lemon and basil (promotes clear thinking)
    - chamomile and lavender (promotes relaxation)
    - orange, lemon and frankincense (stimulates you).

  You can also use essential oils in your bath, a facial mist or your shampoo. To help you get a good night's sleep, add a few drops to your pillow.

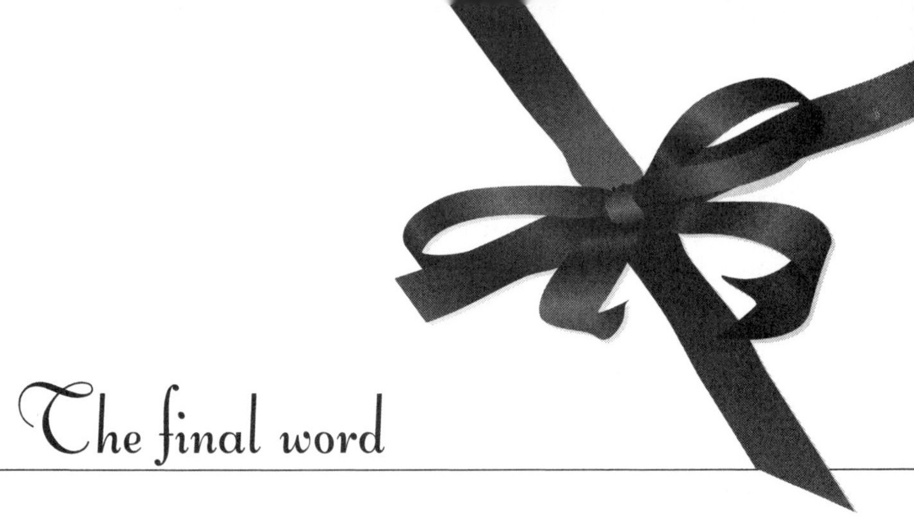

The final word

I hope that you have managed to absorb some of the tips from this book and incorporate them into your weekly routine. It takes only one small step to make a change, but it is essential that you do it.

I want to remind you of the importance of having a support group. Certainly one of the most important things in my life is having the support of my family and friends. I don't mean just having someone who can jump in and look after the kids; having someone who can lend an ear when you really need it most is also critical.

Having a supportive group of friends and siblings (some of whom are now parents) has definitely changed my life. The friends who have stayed with me, particularly after the birth of my two sons, are invaluable to me.

Looking back at the best times in my life, I have always spent these moments with friends. The book club is one example — as is the investment club that followed. I have gained lifelong friends from being with these groups, along with memories of sharing many funny moments.

Just one good friend is worth her weight in gold. You need someone who can join you for a morning walk, or a sensitive friend who will provide an ear to listen to you when you've had a sleepless night with a child. Even having a good friend who will remind that you are working too hard and need to take some time for yourself is a good thing.

Your role as a mum makes you a central figure in your family, so you owe it to yourself to value your role. Allow some time to indulge — your health and your family will be glad you did.

My wish is that once you have read this book, you will take time out for yourself, even if it is just to step back and pat yourself on the back. I have to admit that I've learned a lesson or two about balance over the years. Since writing this book, I have made it a priority to find time to do some of the things that bring me joy. I've made time for beauty treatments and even catching up with friends (and we don't just talk about work or the kids).

To help you do something for yourself, the appendix gives you the chance to write down all the things you would like to do for yourself. Make sure you schedule in at least one purely joyful activity every week.

In fact, I would like all mothers to put aside one day and declare it a national day of beauty for mums everywhere, so that we can take time out to revitalise, refresh and reward ourselves.

So it is on this note that I leave you: support each other and look after yourself, literally!

If you would like to drop me a line, email me at <emily.chantiri@bigpond.com> or visit <www.themoneyclub.com.au>.

Appendix

Rewards for you

Make a list below of all the things that bring you joy. Incorporate them into your daily life, and you'll begin to feel more refreshed in mind, body and spirit.

1 ______________________________

____

2 ______________________________

____

3 ______________________________

____

4 ______________________________

____

5 ______________________________

____

6 ______________________________

____

7 ______________________________

____

8 ______________________________

____

9 ______________________________

____

10 ______________________________

____

11 ______________________________

____

12 ______________________________

____

13 ______________________________

____

14 ______________________________

____

15 ______________________________

____

16 ______________________________

____

17 ______________________________

____

18 ______________________________

____

19 ______________________________

____

20 ______________________________

____

Index

1st for Women Insurance Agency 56

Age Cheap Eats, The 91
Association of Superannuation Funds (ASF) 152
ATMs 2
—fees 4–5
Australian Bankers' Association (ABA) 4
Australian Securities Exchange (ASX) 143
Australian Shareholders' Association (ASA) 143
Australian Shopaholic's Guide to Buying Online, The 21

baby bonus 111–112
bank accounts 3–6
—fees 3–6, 11
—kids' 106

bank accounts (*cont'd*)
—online saving accounts 11–12
—unlimited transactions 4
—withdrawals 3
BankWest 14, 106
beauty treatments, saving on 26–28
—beauty colleges 26
Biotherm 22
budgeting 2–3
BYO restaurants 91

Cannex 50, 56
car insurance, saving on 55–57, 115
cars, saving on 53–58
—car auctions 54
—car-sale websites 54
Chanel 22
children's expenses, reducing 95–96, 109–117
—discounted medication 116
—free activities 113–114
—free video and DVD hire 115
—school shoes 114
—second-hand school uniforms 116–117
—yearly passes 115
CHOICE 3, 5

Christmas savings 84–88
—Kris Kringle 85
Clarins 22
clothes and accessories, saving on 121–137
—annual clothing budget 129
—buying clothes in dark colours 130
—buying on impulse 129
—buying on sale 129
—choosing quality over quantity 120
—clothes parties 133
—designer labels 123–125
—discount clothing websites 131–132
—dry-cleaning costs 127–128
—factory-outlet stores 130
—ironing 127
—making clothes and accessories 134–135

Clothing Can Make A Difference 123
Coca-Cola 81
cosmetics savings 21–30
coupons and catalogues 81–82
credit card debt *see* debt reduction
credit card reward programs 44–48
—frequent flyer programs 45–46
currency conversion 62–63
—American Express travellers' cheques 62
—ATMs overseas 62–63

day of beauty 122
debit cards 50–51
debt reduction 35–52
—credit cards 42–50
-cash withdrawal 49
-checking statements 50
-comparisons 50
-extending limits 48–49
-fee negotiation 49
-interest 43–44, 84–85
-payments 49
-recording purchases 49
—mortgages 35–37
debt versus savings 44
Domino's Pizza 82

eBay 40, 111, 132
education expenses, saving for children's 106–109
—Australian Scholarships Group (ASG) 107
—education saving plans 107–108
-Australian Unity 108
-Commonwealth Bank 108
—private school subsidies 108–109
empowerment 32–33
energy saving 66, 69–74
—air conditioning 70
—energy-efficiency star ratings 73
—standby mode 71–72
—washing 72
entertainment savings 89–92
exercise 162, 164–167
expenses, reducing discretionary 1–17
—coffee 7
—lunches 6
—magazine subscriptions 6
—movie tickets 9, 112

Family Tax Benefits A and B 112
fixed-term deposits 13–14

Grays Online 83, 91
groceries, saving on 78–83
—alcohol 91
—ALDI 79–80
—bulk buying 72, 78

hair products and treatments, saving on 28–30
—hairdressing colleges 29–30
health insurance, reducing the cost of 170–172
hiring help 86–89
holidays 58–63
—airfare discounts 61
—discount travel websites 61–62
—house swapping 58–60
—travelling during school terms 60–61
home, earning income from a 38–42
—boarders 38–40
—letting out a garage 40
—letting to film and production studios 41–42
home, how to save on the 65–92
home loans
—fees and penalties 38
—honeymoon rates 37
—selecting 37–38

immunisation allowance 112
income protection cover 172–173
Income Tax Assessment Act 1997 108
investing 139–157
—cash-management accounts 147–148
—for children 104–106
—managed funds 146–147
—principles 140–144
-educating yourself 141, 142–143
-investment profile 141, 143–144
-planning 141, 141–142
—property 148–150
—shares 145
investment clubs 154–157

lay-by 85

make-up tricks 25, 28
Maybelline 23
McCartney, Stella 124
meditation 168
milestones 37
Money Club, The 155, 156
money management, teaching children 95–117
—accountability and responsibility 99
—explaining investment 102–104
—pocket money 100
—rewards for saving 101
—talking about money 98–99
mortgage brokers 38
mortgage debt *see* debt reduction

Oil of Olay 22

petrol 57–58
phones, saving on 75–78
—billing flexibility 78
—capped and prepaid plans 76–77
—phone messaging 77
—phone providers 77–78
Pilates 169
planning, importance of 6
prioritisation 89
Private Fleet 55

Reserve Bank of Australia (RBA) 4
Revlon 23
rewards, importance of 19–20, 30–33, 71, 92–93, 122, 128, 161–162, 175–177
Rimmel 23

saving 10–15
—saving challenge 14–15
second-hand goods 74–75
Sheba Investment Network (SIN) 155
Shop-A-Dockets 57, 81
Shopping for Shares 143
shopping online 20–21, 83
superannuation 151–154
—co-contributions 153
—employer contributions 152–153
—lost superannuation 154
—voluntary contributions 152–153
support groups 175–176

Target 124
Trading Post 111
treats 15–16, 33, 51–52, 64, 93–94, 118–119, 136–137, 158–159, 173–174

Vera Wang 125
Virgin credit card 43
vitamins and health products, saving on 163
—free health services 163–164
vouchers *see* coupons and catalogues

water saving 66–69
—devices 67–68
—practices 68–69
<www.aussiehouseswap.com.au> 60
<www.buckscoop.com.au> 83
<www.budgetdirect.com.au> 56
<www.dealsdirect.com.au> 83
<www.designeronline.com.au> 131
<www.discountvitaminsexpress.com.au> 163
<www.glamourgirl.com.au> 131–132
<www.graysonline.com.au> 83
<www.homeexchange.com> 60
<www.hotelclub.com.au> 62
<www.houseswap.com> 60
<www.infochoice.com.au> 44
<www.justcarinsurance.com.au> 56
<www.kidsbits.com.au> 113
<www.lastminute.com.au> 62
<www.needitnow.com.au> 62
<www.octopustravel.com> 62
<www.oo.com.au> 83
<www.perfume.com.au> 21
<www.pharmacydirect.com.au> 21
<www.salesguide.com.au> 132
<www.thehealthandbeautyclub.com.au> 21
<www.thexton.com.au> 163
<www.toysonline.com.au> 113
<www.twodollars.com.au> 113
<www.wotif.com> 62

yoga 169

If you found this book useful …

…then you might like to know about other similar books published by John Wiley & Sons. For more information visit our website <www.johnwiley.com.au/trade>, or if you would like to be sent more details about other books in related areas, please photocopy and return the completed coupon below to:

P/T Info
John Wiley & Sons Australia, Ltd
155 Cremorne Street
Richmond Vic 3121

If you prefer you can reply via email to:
<aus_pt_info@johnwiley.com.au>.

Please send me information about books in the following areas of interest:

- ❒ sharemarket (Australian)
- ❒ sharemarket (global)
- ❒ property/real estate
- ❒ taxation and superannuation
- ❒ general business.

Name:
Address:
Email:

Please note that your details will not be added to any mailing list without your consent.